CONSTRUCTING GREEN LANTERN

FROM PAGE to SCREEN

UNIVERSE

First published in the United States of America in 2011 by
Universe Publishing, a division of
Rizzoli International Publications, Inc.
300 Park Avenue South
New York, NY 10010
www.rizzoliusa.com

2011 2012 2013 2014 2015 / 10 9 8 7 6 5 4 3 2

DC Comics Editors: Chris Cerasi and Steve Korte
Universe Editor: Jessica Fuller

Printed in China

Library of Congress Control Number: 2011920264

ISBN-13: 978-0-7893-2261-6

CONSTRUCTING GREEN LANTERN

FROM PAGE to SCREEN

BY OZZY INGUANZO

INTRODUCTION BY GEOFF JOHNS

DESIGN BY CHRIS McDONNELL

UNIVERSE

NEW YORK

ACKNOWLEDGMENTS

My appreciation to Martin Campbell, Donald De Line, Ngila Dickson, Geoff Johns, and Grant Major for their contribution and encouragement. And a heartfelt thanks to Geoff for saying yes—there simply is no one better suited to write this introduction.

To Shane Thompson at Warner Bros., Chris Cerasi and Steve Korté at DC Comics, and Jessica Fuller at Rizzoli for entrusting me with this book. Special thanks to Chris McDonnell for delivering a classy design while in the midst of welcoming a newborn.

To François Audouy, for his unfailing generosity. And to Rodolfo Damaggio, Seth Engstrom, Fabian Lacey, Michele Moen, and Justin Sweet, for their brilliant artwork and support.

To Dava Whisenant, for her constant and invaluable help and encouragement.

Many thanks to Richie Alonzo, Alex Bicknell, Steve Buscaino, Tangi Crawford, Spencer Douglas, François Duhamel, Robert Fechtman, Michael Goldenberg, Matt Gamboa, Collin Grant, Leah Hardstack, Joel Harlow, Joe Hiura, Amanda Hunter, William Hunter, Andrew Jones, Kerry Joseph, Jeff Julian, Anne Kuljian, David Labich, James Lima, Wright McFarland, Paul Ozzimo, Neville Page, Rosa Palomo, Drew Petrotta, Brett Phillips, Eric Ramsey, Kyle Robinson, Constantine Sekeris, Ben Silverman, Aaron Sims, Karl Strahlendorf, and Svetlana Tesnes.

To my parents, Osvaldo and Juanita Inguanzo for their unconditional love and wisdom. Additional thanks to Veronique Audouy, Grant Curtis, Chris Goodnow, Alvin Sargent, Carlene Tiedemann, Heide Waldbaum, and Jorge Yazji.

And to Hal Jordan, for being a constant reminder that we all have within us the ability to overcome fear.

This book is dedicated to the cast and crew of
Green Lantern . . .

And to comic book fans and movie geeks
everywhere.

"What are you afraid of? People like to ask me that. When they do, they have this knowing grin on their faces. As if they expect me to answer, 'nothing.' They think I was born without fear. They're wrong. They think this ring gives me the power to do anything. They're wrong about that too. Before I was given the greatest weapon in the universe, before I journeyed to the stars, my dad gave me the power to do anything. He told me I could be whatever I wanted to be. And I wanted to be just like him."

–Hal Jordan, *Secret Origin*

CONTENTS

→ ESTABLISH vast hall full of GLs.

DIGITAL ① Wide panning Hal + Tomar into the Great Hall

② Sli low angle - 2/S · Hal + Tomar · (Le to Ri)
Hal looks - 3 beats - looks another eyeline - reaching to

DIGITAL - ②A 3 REACTION SHOTS - GLs.

③ C.S Hal + MCS Hal

④ MCS Tomar - watching his reaction.

⑤ Sinestro's entrance - crane down with him - track round be

Match
low
angles
⑥ low angle W/S Sinestro (Ri to te) - Full GL Symbol in

⑦ low angle · Ti MS · (See GL symbol on suit)

DIGITAL - ⑧ very wide shot - From behind - GL symbol + Sinestro POF.

⑨ 2/S Fav Hal - he looks at Group of GLs

DIGITAL ⑩ Group shot GLs (Part of 25) - lower their heads in silen

⑪ low angle

                    TOMAR-RE (V.O.)
          Duration is keyed to one's home
          planet's rotation -- so in your
          case, twenty-four of your hours.

EXT. THE GREAT HALL   *Sinestro's altitude waving just left   70
                              the Guardians.

A canyon FILLED with granite-like PLATFORMS. In the far
distance we can see a giant CENTRAL BATTERY, radiating
green energy and light. Hal stares in wonder.

As they approach the platforms we see standing on them
are hundreds of GREEN LANTERNS. Some big, some small --
all formidable. In the distance is a high, empty
platform, beneath a huge, ancient LANTERN SYMBOL.

Tomar and Hal land on a platform overlooking the meeting.

                              *Hal is gobsmacked by the spectacle of 3600 GLs
                    HAL   - then he locks on to 2 reactions:
          There's so many.

Hal stares out at the astonishing collection of
creatures. Some are still landing around them.

                    TOMAR-RE - hes seen this bewilderment before.
          The stars you can see from your
          home planet, on the clearest
          night: your Sector is a thousand
          times larger. And 3600 Lanterns,
          each with a sector just as vast... *-Hal looks up at the approaching
                                                              Sinestro.

As Hal tries to absorb the unbelievable scale of that
information, a dramatic figure -- SINESTRO -- lands on
the empty platform. A hush falls over the assembly.

                    SINESTRO
          Khen-To. Avira. Fentara. Abin-
          Sur.
               (quietly) thinking of Abin
          A moment of silence for our fallen
          comrades. *Hal looks at a group lowering their eyes

The huge hall falls silent, each Lantern lost in his own
memories. Then Sinestro speaks again.

                    SINESTRO
          I've called you here, to this
          unprecedented gathering, because
          we face an unprecedented danger.
          Our four Lantern brothers were
unusual and - killed by an enemy called Parallax
very serious   -- an enemy we don't yet fully
          understand.
                    (MORE)

INTRODUCTION

"You have the ability to overcome fear."

There's not a single phrase, beyond the iconic Green Lantern oath, that I've typed more often when writing *Green Lantern* these last eight years. Be it from Green Lantern's ring or his fellow Corps members, overcoming fear is the essential quality within every sentient being chosen from across the universe to join the ranks of the Guardians' emerald intergalactic police force. For me, it's the very heart of what Green Lantern is all about and as human beings it is an ability we all possess.

Director Martin Campbell, producer Donald De Line and the film-makers and writers of the film embraced that theme of overcoming fear throughout the production, figuratively and literally. They not only stayed true to the core of Green Lantern, they explored the mythology and brought it to life in ways I have dreamed of since I was eight years old. And they did one hell of a job.

When I first learned that director Martin Campbell, who had re-invented both Zorro and James Bond with great success critically and commercially, had signed on for *Green Lantern* I immediately knew this film was in the perfect hands. Martin knows how to tap into the soul of a decades-loved character and celebrate everything they were, are and will be thanks to him. Watching him direct Ryan Reynolds and Mark Strong as they confront one another on the planet of Oa was *the* single greatest experience in my career.

And let's talk about the cast that Donald De Line and crew assembled. Ryan Reyonds as Hal Jordan, Mark Strong as Sinestro, Blake Lively as Carol Ferris, and Peter Sarsgaard as Hector Hammond.

Ryan is absolutely the perfect Hal Jordan and, being a comic fan himself, he always wanted to get it "right." With his intense power and quick wit, he did.

Mark was insistent on the make-up being faithful to the character of Sinestro, whom he played brilliantly. Every glimpse of him is utterly captivating.

Determined to bring both strength and care to Carol Ferris, Blake was also adamant about dying her blonde hair to match the darker color of Carol from the comics.

And Peter was a constant professional—despite the grueling hours of make-up in the New Orleans heat—who elevated an arguably minor villain in the Green Lantern mythology to a truly complex, emotional, and nuanced character far beyond anything anyone expected.

In the pages ahead, you'll see just how much work, talent, and passion went into bringing one of the greatest comic book heroes ever

created to life. Author Ozzy Inguanzo, designer Chris McDonnell, and editors Chris Cerasi and Steve Korté have put together the definitive look at the production with *Constructing Green Lantern: From Page to Screen.*

And before I wrap this up so you can enjoy this amazing book, I have to also give a special personal thanks to Ozzy, the author, who also helped maintain the attention to detail and concept throughout the entire production of the film with DC Entertainment. His dedication and passion for the source material helped insure the accuracy throughout the production—from the major elements like Parallax to the visuals of Amanda Waller's past ripped straight from the pages of the comics. Fanboys everywhere should thank him for that forever. I do.

Enjoy the book!

In Brightest Day, In Blackest Night—

Geoff Johns

Los Angeles, California
January 2011

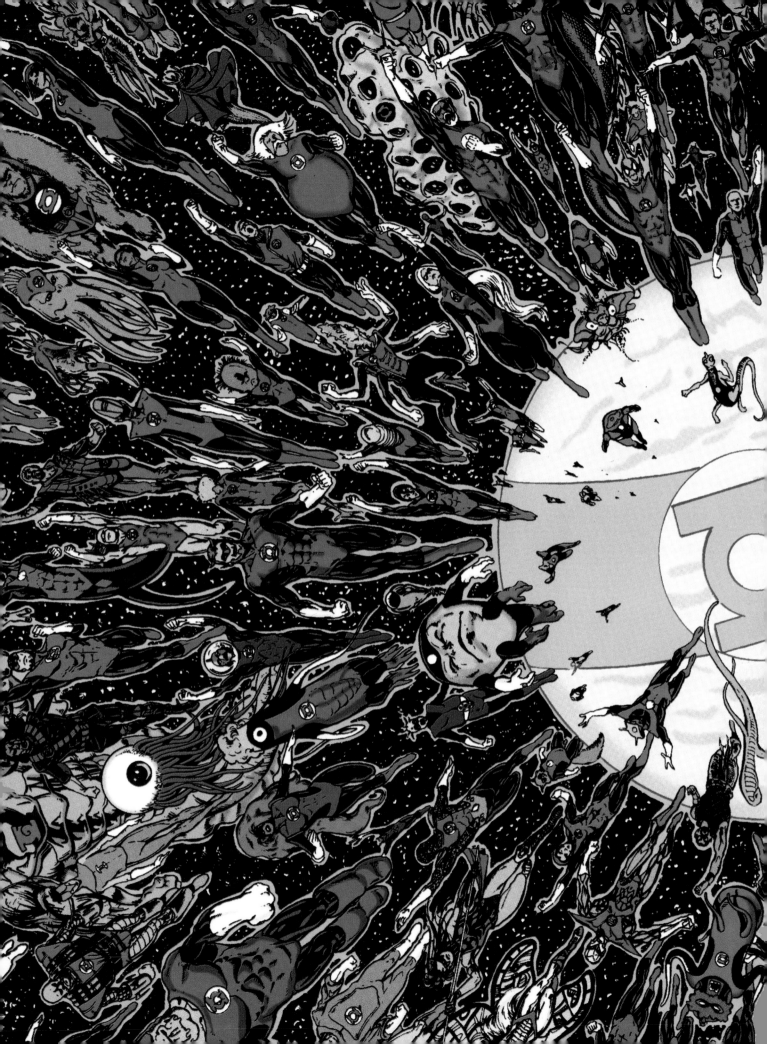

Above: *DC Comics revamped the Green Lantern, reintroducing the character to a new generation of space age readers on this front cover of* Showcase *no. 22 (September 1959). Art by Gil Kane.*

FROM SILVER AGE TO SILVER SCREEN

Below: *Alan Scott as Green Lantern leaps into action on the cover of* Green Lantern *no. 1 (Fall 1941). He was given his own title after his debut in* All-American Comics *no. 16 (July 1940). His costume changed quite a bit when the character was revived in 1959. Art by Howard Purcell.*

Pages 12–13: *Green Lanterns from all sectors of the universe fly into action in this classic image from* Green Lantern Gallery *(1996). Art by Phil Jimenez.*

Falling fast from the sky, a small alien spacecraft crashes in a desolate area near the Southwestern coast of North America. Within the vessel, a mortally wounded alien warrior with magenta skin engages his green Power Ring. He must locate the nearest suitable replacement to whom he can impart his "battery of power," his green lantern. The ring selects Hal Jordan, an unsuspecting test pilot with the ability to overcome great fear. He is bestowed with the powers and responsibilities of the intergalactic patrolman and adopts the name Green Lantern.

That legendary origin story, conceived in the late 1950s, was not the birth of the Green Lantern but a reinterpretation. Created by illustrator Mark Nodell and written by Bill Finger, the character previously debuted during the height of the Golden Age of comics in the July 1940 publication *All-American Comics* No. 16.

Like many super heroes of that time, the Green Lantern's supernatural abilities came from a mystical source. In the case of railroad engineer Alan Scott: a lantern with a magical green flame came into his possession following a railroad accident. Scott forged a Power Ring from the lantern's metal and became the mighty crime fighter of the same name.

By the late 1940s, interest in super-hero comics was fading and DC Comics was forced to cancel several series, including Alan Scott's Green Lantern adventures. The Golden Age of comics had come to an end.

With the dawn of the space age approaching, DC Comics editor Julius Schwartz saw an opportunity to revive the company's once famous stable of Golden Age super heroes by reimagining them for burgeoning science fiction fans. After successfully relaunching the Flash in 1956, DC selected Schwartz to breathe new life into Green Lantern. He enlisted writer John Broome and illustrator Gil Kane, and in October of 1959 a spaceman by the name of Abin Sur bequeathed his Power Ring and lantern to Hal Jordan of Earth, ushering Green Lantern into the Silver Age of comics and beyond.

Much like the lantern itself, the legacy of the comic continues to burn brightly. The many talented writers and artists chosen as its stewards over the years have built upon and expanded the hero's cosmic mythology,

passing it on for subsequent generations to do the same. Through comics, books, toys, video games, and animated films, the Green Lantern has been a mainstay in popular culture; but a feature film version starring the Emerald Warrior would not land in theaters until 2011. Almost one half-century after the character's sci-fi debut in *Showcase* No. 22, Warner Bros. Pictures and DC Entertainment would release the first live-action feature film adaptation of the Green Lantern.

With *Casino Royale* and *Zorro* director Martin Campbell at the helm and Donald De Line producing, early conceptual design on the film began in February 2009. "We wanted to design a world that was visually stunning and yet credible, while still maintaining the spirit of the comics," explains De Line. They assembled a stellar team of talented artists and filmmakers under the direction of Academy Award-winning production and costume designers of *The Lord of the Rings*, Grant Major and Ngila Dickson, and the Academy Award-winning cinematographer of *Memoirs Of A Geisha*, Dion Beebe.

The journey began in Burbank 2 1/2 years prior to the film's release, and took the filmmakers to Melbourne, Sydney, New Orleans, and beyond the stars, all the way to the center of the universe in an effort finally to translate the Green Lantern from the Silver Age to the silver screen.

Above: *In this image from the film, Abin Sur imparts his Power Ring to unsuspecting pilot Hal Jordan, sealing his fate as the next protector of Space Sector 2814.*

Right: *The fateful encounter within the pages of the debut issue,* Showcase *no. 22 (September 1959). Text by John Broome and art by Gil Kane and Joe Giella.*

Pages 18–19: *The Power Ring. Photo by François Duhamel.*

STARTLED, THE CRACK TEST PILOT ENTERS THE WRECKED SHIP...

I AM *ABIN SUR*... I AM NOT OF EARTH--BUT OF A FAR DISTANT PLANET--AND I AM... DYING...

HOW CAN I HELP--

NO...IT IS TOO LATE TO HELP ME... BESIDES, I MUST SPEAK TO YOU... OF A MORE IMPORTANT MATTER...

MORE IMPORTANT... THAN YOUR *LIFE?*

YES...LOOK AT THIS *BATTERY,* HAL JORDAN...

WHY...IT LOOKS LIKE A *GREEN LANTERN...*

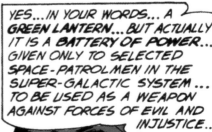

YES...IN YOUR WORDS... A *GREEN LANTERN*...BUT ACTUALLY IT IS A *BATTERY OF POWER*... GIVEN ONLY TO SELECTED SPACE-PATROLMEN IN THE SUPER-GALACTIC SYSTEM... TO BE USED AS A WEAPON AGAINST FORCES OF EVIL AND INJUSTICE...

IT IS OUR DUTY...WHEN DISASTER STRIKES... TO PASS ON THE *BATTERY OF POWER*... TO ANOTHER WHO IS *FEARLESS*... AND *HONEST!* COME CLOSER TO ME...

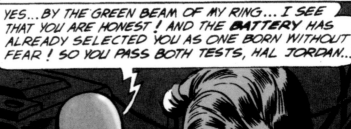

YES...BY THE GREEN BEAM OF MY RING... I SEE THAT YOU ARE HONEST! AND THE *BATTERY* HAS ALREADY SELECTED YOU AS ONE BORN WITHOUT FEAR! SO YOU PASS BOTH TESTS, HAL JORDAN...

Above: *Director Martin Campbell (left) and production designer Grant Major review construction drawings on set. Photo by François Duhamel.*

Near right: Green Lantern: Rebirth *was originally published in 2004 as a six-issue miniseries written by Geoff Johns. Cover art by Ethan Van Sciver.*

Far right: *Writer Geoff Johns revisits Green Lantern's origins in* Green Lantern: Secret Origin. *This compilation of issues 29–35 was the most widely referenced book by the filmmakers. Cover art by Ivan Reis and Dave McCaig.*

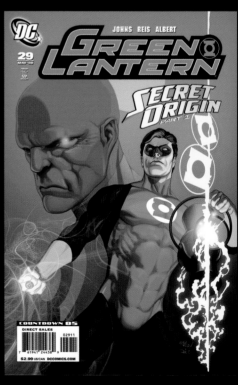

VISUAL DEVELOPMENT

Translating a comic book into a live-action feature-length film is always challenging, and anyone who's familiar with the Green Lantern comic book universe knows that in order to remain faithful to the books, any adaptation would need to be uniquely epic in cosmic scope. Additionally, in order for the comic's fantastical elements to work on film, they would need to feel tangible and plausible to the audience.

Early in the film's development, director Martin Campbell began by fostering visuals that grounded the story. "You really have to take the material deadly serious. It's no different than doing Hamlet; in fact [it's] more difficult in some ways in that you have to give it a reality in order to make the fantasy credible. Here's a guy in a green suit that's been chosen and flown to a planet at the center of the universe courtesy of a ring, basically. So there has to be a logic to the world that you create, otherwise the whole thing can spin out of control," explains Campbell.

As production designer Grant Major recalls, "The art department was a tool for [Martin Campbell] to develop and visualize ideas, and he wanted as much access to us as possible." Exactly one year prior to commencing principal photography, Major—along with supervising art director François Audouy and a team of conceptual artists—moved the *Green Lantern* art department out of the Warner Bros. studio lot in Burbank and into the Tribeca West complex on the west side of Los Angeles. Working off an early draft of the film's screenplay by Greg Berlanti, Michael Green, and Marc Guggenheim, they set up shop just above Campbell's office, where the director was putting the finishing touches on his previous film, the Mel Gibson thriller *Edge of Darkness*.

A thorough study of the comics began immediately; research spanning nearly fifty years of source material. The film focused on a selection of stories, primarily writer Geoff Johns's reintroduction of the Hal Jordan character in *Rebirth*, *No Fear*, and *Secret Origin*. Also referenced were the early 1960s comics by John Broome, specifically *Green Lantern* No. 40, as well as the *Emerald Dawn* series from the 1980s, and even the recent *Tales of the Sinestro Corps* and *The Sinestro Corps Wars*. Historical biographies were written up on all the characters and environments, along

Above: *Comic book panel from* Green Lantern Secret Origin. *Art by Ivan Reis.*

with images of their various comic interpretations throughout the years. Research was also conducted on a diverse range of aesthetics in the arts and sciences, which Major mined for inspiration. He would then give selected reference images and preliminary pencil sketches to the concept artists who developed and visualized them into beautifully rendered paintings.

Several times per week, Campbell, along with producer Donald De Line, would assemble key players involved with the film's visual development to review and workshop concepts. "It's very empowering when it's inclusive like that right from the beginning. He really let us go for it," says the production designer. The seasoned director would sit at the head of the conference room table and engage them on every aspect of the narrative, challenging them to come up with never-before-seen visuals, and listening as they pitched their ideas. "I've always been a great believer in letting the artists run free. They've read the script; they have their own ideas, let them start to develop them—and certainly in this case, working with Grant, they came up with some marvelous stuff," says Campbell.

Concept artist James Lima, who was known for his occasional wild ideas, recognizes Campbell's years of experience and confidence. "It was like being in the sure hands of Obi-Wan Kenobi," he quips. Fellow concept

Top: *Director Martin Campbell (right) runs through the Ferris Party sequence with (left to right) supervising art director François Audouy, production designer Grant Major, and second unit director John Mahaffie. Photo by Ozzy Inguanzo.*

Above left: *Director Martin Campbell presides over an early visual development meeting in Los Angeles. Photo by Ozzy Inguanzo.*

Above right: *Green Lantern's director's chair on set. Photo by Ozzy Inguanzo.*

artist Rodolfo Damaggio continues, "Everything was discussed openly, and even some far-out concepts were indulged. The ones selected would then go on to further development."

The illustrations that gained traction would immediately be red-stamped for security "ART DEPT. DO NOT COPY," and pinned up on the wall for all to see. Eventually, the gallery outgrew the confines of the conference room, and extended into the lengthy corridor. In time, a cohesive vision of the film began to emerge, laying the groundwork for the detailed architectural drawings and 3-D models required to build the digital and functional sets, props, vehicles, and environments.

Getting them built on time and on budget largely fell on construction coordinator John Hoskins, who oversaw a team of approximately 175 crew: multiple foremen, carpenters, plasterers, mold makers, painters, sculptors, welders, and laborers. On the digital front, visual effects supervisors Kent Houston and John "D.J." Des Jardin, visual effects producer Alex Bicknell, and Sony Pictures Imageworks' visual effects supervisor Jim Berney headed a team of hundreds of artists, including animators, modelers, texture artists, and lighting technicians.

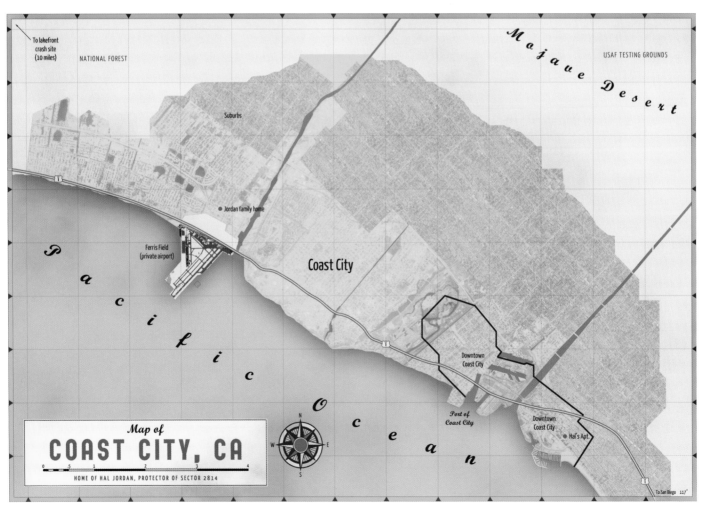

WELCOME TO COAST CITY, CA

Top left: *Fabian Lacey used an aerial photo he took while descending into Los Angeles as the foundation for this concept illustration of Coast City.*

Bottom left: *This map of Coast City denotes the geographical location of certain sets within the fictional city. Map by François Audouy with Rosa Palomo.*

Within the pages of the DC comic book universe, far west of Batman's Gotham City, Flash's Central City, and Superman's Metropolis, and stretching along the Pacific Ocean in Southern California, you'll find the fictional Coast City. Popular for its sunny, arid climate and beautiful beaches, Coast City prides itself on its rich heritage in the aerospace industry, but more importantly, it is known as the home to Earth's first Green Lantern, Hal Jordan.

There are several geographical and architectural components that constitute the most famous Southern California coastal cities, such as San Diego, Santa Monica, and Long Beach. Production designer Grant Major wanted to fuse all of those elements together to design the ultimate Coast City. As concept designer Fabian Lacey recalls, "Grant came to me with a basket full of research images. It had to have a downtown city close to the desert, bordered by mountains that were on a crescent harbor, with a port and warehouse district on the south side, and the Ferris airport further north off the coast. The whole city was designed from the inside out." Flying into Los Angeles one afternoon, Lacey looked out his window and snapped a photograph of Santa Monica harbor. "It was a beautiful eye level that we don't really get to see too much. I then did a quick paint over to incorporate some of the design elements we had discussed."

Although Southern California seems like it would be an ideal location to shoot the film, it was largely cost prohibitive. In an effort to keep production costs low, many film productions gravitate toward locations that offer competitive tax incentives; *Green Lantern* was no different. Initially the filmmakers had scouted both Melbourne and Sydney and seemed committed to shooting there; but by late July 2009, due to the rapidly declining exchange rate of the U.S. dollar, Warner Bros. began serious discussions about pulling *Green Lantern* out of Australia. They scoured the United States for locations: Louisiana, Michigan, New Mexico and Massachusetts were considered. At one point even New Zealand and South Africa were discussed as options.

"One of the top choices from the very beginning was Louisiana, but it was important to remember that this film takes place in a fictional part

of Southern California, and many of the scenes play out at Ferris Aircraft. We desperately needed to find a location with an airport nearby," explains supervising art director François Audouy. After doing a quick search online for World War II era airports in Louisiana, he recalls the eureka moment when he came upon Lakefront Airport, "I was like, 'It's on the lake! It's on the water! They're restoring the art deco main terminal building!'"

Lakefront Airport, located on the south side of the great Lake Pontchartrain, seemed perfect, but it was undergoing a massive reconstruction effort. During the Cold War in the 1960s, its main terminal building, which was originally built in the late 1930s, had been repurposed as a fallout shelter. For nearly half a century, its art deco architecture was covered up with a minimalist and uninspiring exterior shell consisting of thick reinforced concrete slabs. In 2005, it was devastated by the effects of Hurricane Katrina. The building, along with most of its surrounding hangars, was still heavily damaged by the time crewmembers began arriving in New Orleans.

Although the renovation was already under way, Audouy remembers that there was no guarantee it would be completed in time for filming. "The first thing airport officials told us was that they might be able to have the back, lake-side, of the terminal building ready by filming, but that we'd never be able photograph the land side of the building because it would never be done in time. Of course, we ended up having one of our biggest scenes featuring the land-side of the terminal building, and ultimately shot almost every corner of that airport."

Finding large enough studio space was also essential. Unfortunately the new state-of-the-art sound stages at New Orleans's Second Line Stages weren't quite ready either. When the company opened their New Orleans production offices in October 2009, the stages were still under basic construction. One of the first local hires, set designer Wright McFarland, recalls his first impression when he was sent to survey the stages, "The idea that it would be a completed and functional studio in time for filming seemed absolutely ludicrous. They pulled off a remarkable achievement." Ultimately, the filmmakers employed a combination of stage and location filming, along with virtual environments and plate photography, to conjure up Coast City.

Above top: *Photos of Lakefront Airport taken by Grant Major on a location scout of New Orleans in Septemeber 2009.*

Above middle: *Coast City seal. Graphic by Amanda Hunter with Zachary Zirlin.*

Above bottom: *Coast City license plate graphic by Amanda Hunter.*

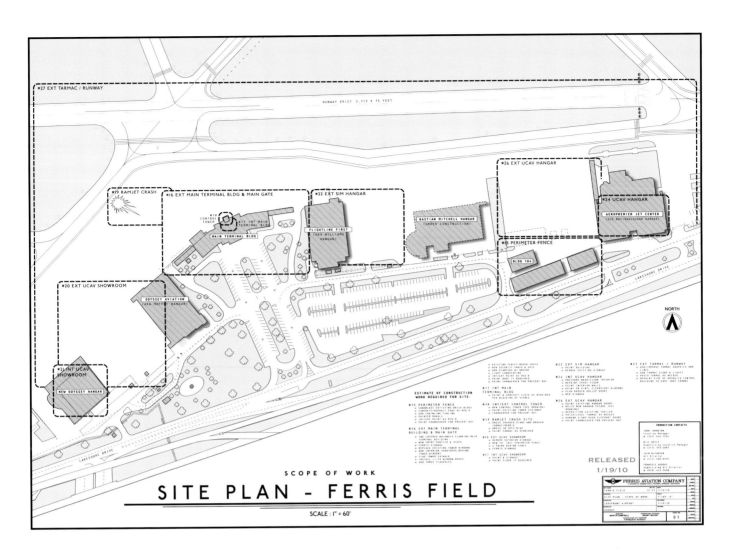

SCOPE OF WORK

SITE PLAN – FERRIS FIELD

SCALE : 1" = 60'

Top: *This scope of work site plan by François Audouy breaks down the construction work required to transform the working Lakefront Airport into the film's fictional Ferris Aircraft.*

Above: *Concept illustrations by Paul Christopher of Ferris Aircraft's main gate, past and present.*

Top left: *Producer Donald De Line with actors Ryan Reynolds and Blake Lively between takes on the first day of principal photography (March 15, 2009) at the Old Point Bar in New Orleans, a local dive which was converted into Broome's Bar for the film. Screenwriter Michael Goldenberg says he turned to Geoff Johns for the name. "I asked if he had any ideas for an appropriate name for this bar I was basing on the test pilot bar in* The Right Stuff. *He suggested "Broome's" as a tribute to comic book writer John Broome, I said perfect, and typed it into the script." Photo by François Duhamel.*

Bottom left: *Hal Jordan and Carol Ferris in Broome's Bar. Photo by François Duhamel.*

Right: *Frames from a Ferris Aircraft corporate video, produced by the art department. It plays on a jumbotron in the Ferris party sequence. Video graphics by Chris Kieffer.*

FERRIS AIRCRAFT

Top left: *Ferris Aircraft as it appears in the early 1990's sequence of the film. Photo by François Duhamel.*

Bottom left: *Inspired by Polish art deco painter Tamara de Lempicka, and celebrating the glory of flight, this digital painting by Fabian Lacey was printed on canvas and treated to resemble a wall mural from the 1930s. It was displayed in the Ferris office set.*

Family owned and operated for more than seventy-five years, Ferris Aircraft plays as pivotal a role in the film as it does in the comics. The aviation company, which employs thousands of Coast City residents, specializes in the design and manufacture of advanced jet fighter platforms for its primary customer, the United States Department of Defense.

To help director Martin Campbell and the filmmakers visualize the scope of Ferris Aircraft, concept artist Rodolfo Damaggio worked closely with production designer Grant Major and supervising art director François Audouy to build a 3-D digital model of the existing Lakefront Airport, which he then extended and incorporated into the Coast City suburbs. "We wanted to show the extent and legacy of Ferris Aircraft, so beyond the actual location, I modeled the aircraft factory, aviation research laboratories, wind tunnels, additional hangars, and other typical buildings. I even took field trips out to Edwards Air Force Base, the Mojave Airport, Miramar, and Chino to take detailed photographs of equipment, textures, and the surrounding desert, which I later applied to the 3-D model. At one point I got into a little hot water at Edwards when they started to become suspicious of all the photos I was taking, but it was for a good cause."

One of the first sets designed on the film belongs to Carl Ferris, the president and owner of Ferris Aircraft. His office—which he hands over to his daughter Carol, along with the keys to the company—features prominently in the story. While the main terminal at Lakefront served as the building's exterior, it also informed some of the interior designs. As assistant art director Robert Fechtman explains, "Whatever the task calls for you come up with a concept based on the research and the location you're trying to match. In this case, Grant wanted to maintain the more simplified Americanized art deco style."

Story and character also serve to inspire the design of a set, as Fechtman elaborates, "It's what generates the color palette, what generates masculine versus feminine. We wanted the ceiling to be high because this character was an important guy, and we wanted to have tall windows, not just to match the location, but because this guy was the head of the company."

Above: *This final concept illustration of
Ferris Aircraft by Fabian Lacey incorporates
a Southern California mountain range into
Rodolfo Damaggio's 3-D model of Ferris,
which was partially based on the existing
Lakefront Airport location in New Orleans.
Set decorator Anne Kuljian even made use
of the image by having it mounted and
placed in Carl Ferris's office.*

Left: *This prop badge, worn by a lowly Ferris UCAV technician, is an example of property master Drew Petrotta's meticulous attention to detail. Graphics by Amanda Hunter with Zachary Zirlin.*

Ferris Aircraft 33

Another important component that is largely overlooked when discussing set design is construction. Fechtman explains, "As a set designer, you need to be grounded in the knowledge of how things are assembled and put together using construction materials. The bare minimum that your construction crew needs from your drawings when building a set, always boils down to: plan, elevation, section, detail."

When Fechtman arrived in New Orleans in November, he had a well-developed set of work drawings for Ferris's office and transferred over the project to art director Iain McFadyen and set designer Wright McFarland, who completed and oversaw construction of the office set at Second Line Stages. As McFarland explains, "All of the design elements in that set were both derived and in some cases lifted from existing art deco elements at Lakefront's terminal building. It was heartening to know that these architectural elements were genuine and not just period-inspired."

A perfectly designed set is empty without the contributions of another key member of the design team, the set decorator. Before leaving to New Orleans, Audouy suggested to Major that he meet with Anne Kuljian, whom Audouy had worked with on director Steven Spielberg's *The Terminal* and *Minority Report*.

One of Kuljian's first assignments was the Ferris office set, which required multiple depictions: Carl's 1993 office, his present-day office, and Carol's office. Having a fictional back-story for the set was important, says Kuljian: "We felt that the family business had started in the 1940s and that Carl had just taken over from his father. So the desk that we see throughout the whole movie, in Carl's office and then in Carol's, that art deco desk would have been the original desk from the original office. Through the years, some of the furniture would have been left over from the '40s, then from the '50s, and then the '60s, and the '70s. By the time you see Carl's 1993 office, it's a hodgepodge of all the past years at Ferris." For Carl's present-day office, the clutter was removed, and the office was given a more sleek corporate look, suggesting a new era at Ferris, when Carl, with Carol by his side, relaunches the company into the future.

Top: *Hangar detail. Photo by Grant Major.*

Above: *Wooden floor pattern and compass rose graphic for the Ferris office set by Amanda Hunter.*

Below: *(left to right) Dion Beebe, John Buckley, and Grant Major discuss the lighting scheme for the Ferris party set. Photo by François Duhamel.*

The use of color also helps inform character and establish mood. "Grant wanted the old '93 office to have much more golden tones, warm woods, and browns. Carol, on the other hand is modern, clean, and cool. So she's grays, pale blues, and silvers," says Kuljian. That contrast helps underscore Carol's influence and involvement at Ferris. Once she moves into her father's office permanently, another visual clue was worked into the set, a detail meant to suggest she's taking the family business into the future by restoring it to its former glory. "The idea was that Carol had the old carpeting removed to reveal the original wooden floor and compass rose from the 1940s office," Kuljian confesses. An ironic twist with reality perhaps, considering the actual Lakefront Airport terminal building on which the set was based was undergoing its own restoration.

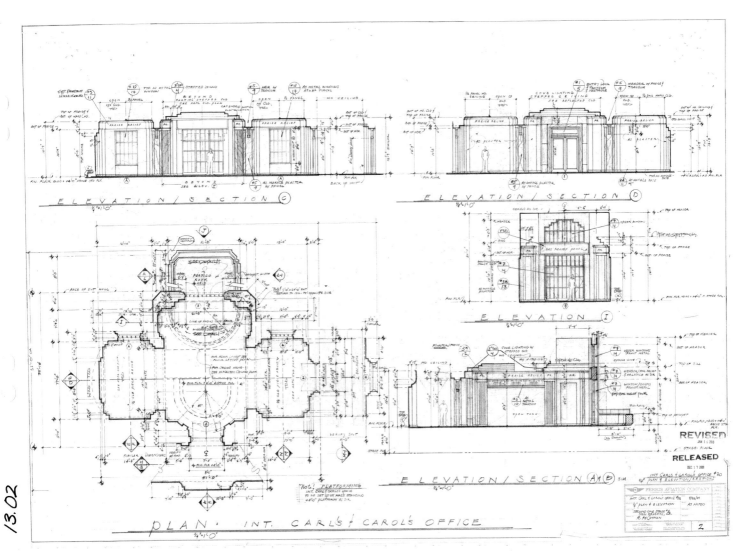

Top left: *Congressman Robert Hammond greets a young Hal Jordan and Carol Ferris in this image of Carl Ferris's office from the early 1990s. Photo by François Duhamel.*

Top right: *Years later, Hal and Carol square off in the same office. Photo by François Duhamel.*

Above: *1/4" plan and elevation for the interior of Carl and Carol Ferris's office by Robert Fechtman.*

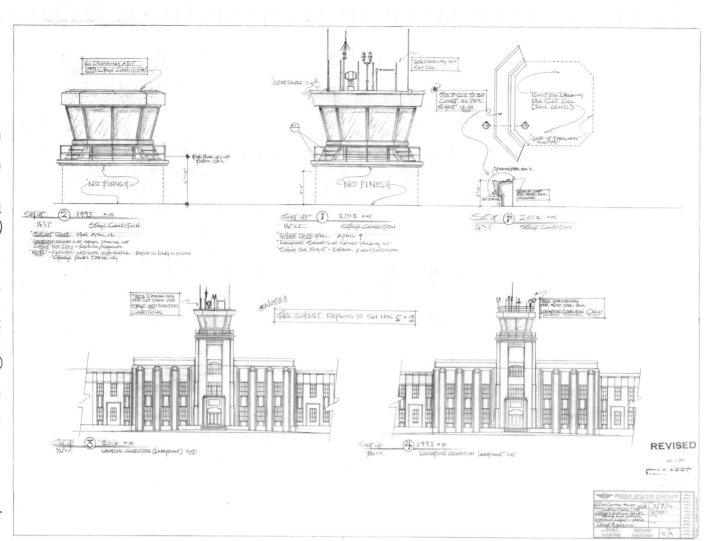

Above: *Interior/Exterior Control Tower cab, stage and location set-ups by Wright McFarland.*

Left: *Control tower set under construction in the parking lot at Second Line Stages. The set was later mounted atop the main terminal building at Lakefront Airport. Photo by Grant Major.*

Opposite: *Conceptual illustration by Fabian Lacey (top right) of a touching character moment between Hal Jordan and Carol Ferris atop the control tower, looking out over Ferris to the Pacific coast in the distance. A two-camera set up of the same scene (bottom right) being shot on a bluescreen stage. Photo by François Duhamel.*

FABIAN LACEY · GREEN LANTERN · FERRIS AIRPORT NIGHT · 01.28.

Above: (top) Hangar that houses Ferris Aircraft's next generation UCAVs and their corresponding Command and Control trailer. Photo by François Duhamel. (bottom) Concept illustration of same by Rodolfo Damaggio.

THE PLANES

Left: *Ferris Aircraft's next generation unmanned combat aerial vehicles, or UCAVs, by Paul Ozzimo.*

Below: *Storyboard panels of the DOGFIGHT sequence by Richard Newsome.*

Two F-35B Lightning II fighter jets—with Hal and Carol at the controls—face off in a high-octane dogfight over the Mojave Desert against two Sabre X-97s; Ferris's next generation unmanned combat aerial vehicles, or UCAVs. Although the sequence is almost entirely computer generated, director Martin Campbell wanted it to be as credible as possible, from the design of the aircraft and their flight maneuvers, to the manner in which it was photographed. To serve as the film's technical advisor, he enlisted retired United States Air Force Colonel Rick Searfoss. The former NASA astronaut and Space Shuttle Commander had also been a flight instructor at the prestigious U.S. Air Force Test Pilot School at Edwards Air Force Base. For months, he assisted Campbell in assembling the sequence with storyboard artist Richard Newsome and pre-visualization supervisor Kyle Robinson.

Production designer Grant Major tapped concept designer Paul Ozzimo to conceive a UCAV that was aggressive, yet met Campbell's criteria. "We kept it in the realm of sci-fact, and based it on existing or current-future technologies. One of its features is a big round fan right through the center of the body. Those do exist now, but we pushed it beyond just hovering and made it useable for flight maneuvers. Also, the bizarre under-over wing geometry might seem a bit odd as well, but it was also based on current experimental trends," explains Ozzimo. His final digital 3-D model, which plays in the sequence, was also reproduced as a full-scale prop for other key scenes in the film.

For Hal and Carol's F-35Bs, the art department provided the entire front cockpit portion of one fighter, doubling for both, which would be mounted on a motion-base and photographed against a bluescreen for close-ups of actors Ryan Reynolds and Blake Lively piloting the vehicles. In October 2009, vehicles art director Karl Strahlendorf headed to the Flight Test Nation Air Show and Open House at Edwards Air Force Base to see the plane up close. The military's next generation multi-role fighter jet was still in its flight-testing phase and didn't make too many public appearances. In fact, this was its first air show appearance. Mostly using photographs, Strahlendorf oversaw its reproduction with Adam Gurley and his team at Wild Factory in Camarillo, CA.

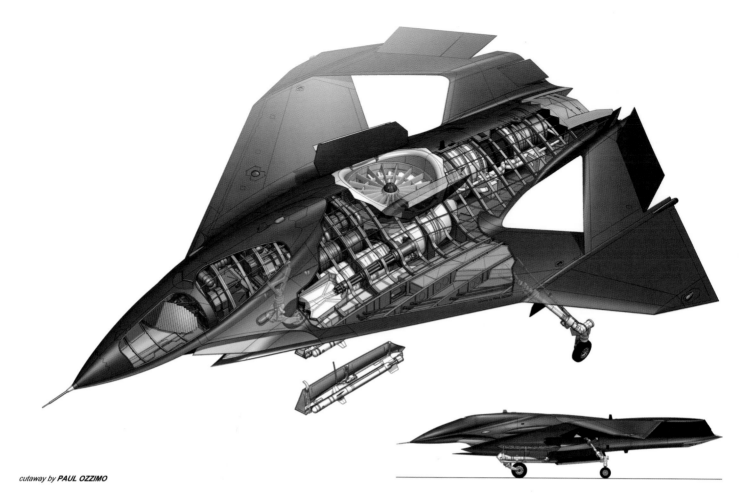

cutaway by **PAUL OZZIMO**

The precursor to Ferris's pilotless X-97 UCAV was their infamous high performance fighter jet from the early 1990s, the YF-32, piloted by Hal's father, Martin Jordan. The jet that ultimately took the life of Hal's father in the film also needed to be designed and built. "I based the shape of the YF-32 on planes like the F-20 Tigershark, the early F-18 Hornet, and a few other odd birds that DARPA (Defense Advanced Research Projects Agency) was playing around with back then. Overall, it might seem a bit conventional until you see the tail. Instead of the traditional vertical fin, we created an early version of what is called the Pelican tail, or the two angled rear stabilizers. That would have been considered very advanced for the mid- to late-1980s," says Ozzimo.

There were three YF-32s built for the film, two full-sized planes and one cockpit section used for certain inserts, as well as close-ups of actor Jon Tenney who portrays the elder Jordan. The production purchased two decommissioned F-5 Tiger jets (minus the engines) and Strahlendorf converted them into Ozzimo's YF-32 design with Mark Visconti and Charlie Zurian at Visconti Engineering in California. "When I was five years old, I had family working at Northrop in Hawthorne, California, and was invited to see the rollout and flight of the F-5. To be able to help turn that very plane into an experimental fighter of my own for the movie was pretty cool," says Ozzimo.

The two full-scale planes arrived from California in pieces and were assembled at Lakefront Airport. One was retrofitted with a cable line and towed down the airport tarmac up to sixty miles per hour with a stunt man sitting in the cockpit in place of Tenney. The other "post-crash" plane was rigged by the film's special effects department for the fiery explosion.

Above: *This cutaway by Paul Ozzimo features the inner workings of the X-97 UCAV and was used as set dressing in Carl Ferris's office.*

Above: *Actress Blake Lively was filmed inside the F-35B mock-up, which was mounted on a motion-base and surrounded by a bluescreen. These elements were then turned over to the visual effects team to complete the illusion of Carol Ferris piloting the fighter jet. Photo by François Duhamel.*

Top right: *The X-97 Sabre on display inside one of Ferris Aircraft's newer hangars. Concept illustration by Fabian Lacey.*

Bottom right: *The full-scale UCAV, rear wings already removed, sits inside the construction workshop just before being transported to Lakefront Airport for the Ferris party sequence. Photo by François Audouy.*

FABIAN LACEY · GREEN LANTERN · UCAV SHOWROOM 01.26.10

Top: *Martin Jordan's test plane clips the control tower on its fiery descent, in this early concept illustration by Alex Laurant. Prior to acquiring the Lakefront Airport location for filming, the control tower was initially conceived as a separate structure.*

Above: *The crew prepares the crashed YF-32 for filming. Photo by Rosa Palomo.*

Left: *Martin Jordan prior to his fateful test flight. Illustration by Paul Christopher.*

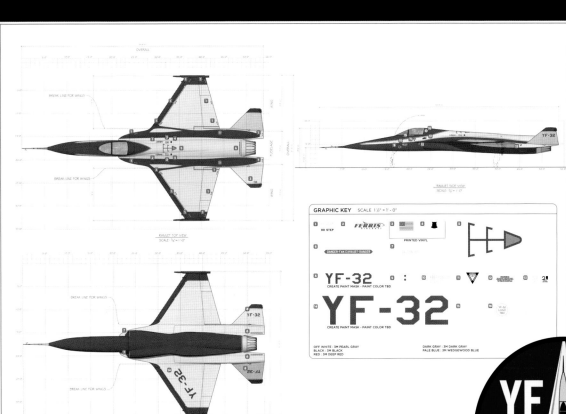

Above: *Post-crash illustration by Paul Ozzimo.*

Left: *Final graphic key for Martin Jordan's test plane. Graphics by Amanda Hunter with Zachary Zirlin.*

Below: *YF-32 test program graphics by Amanda Hunter with Zachary Zirlin.*

CHOOSING HAL

Top and middle left: *Key frame illustrations by Rodolfo Damaggio of young Hal running towards the crash site.*

Bottom left: *The tragic scene as it appears in the film. Photo by François Duhamel.*

Below: *Martin Jordan's obituary hangs in Broome's Bar. Graphics by Amanda Hunter.*

Young Hal's life was irrevocably altered when he witnessed his father perish while piloting Ferris's YF-32 test plane. That tragic image of the young boy on the tarmac wearing his dad's classic leather bomber jacket is meant to resonate throughout the film. Hal's journey to become a true hero like his father, to overcome great fear, requires him to grow physically and emotionally into that jacket.

The jacket's design proved to be a tricky one for costume designer Ngila Dickson. The story required it to be retro, but Dickson was concerned about how it would look on actor Ryan Reynolds in the present-day scenes. "We looked at some really great old leather jackets, but it wasn't until [costumer] Tamsin Costello, brought in her grandfather's flight jacket that it really came together for me. We ended up taking that design and updating it just a bit. It actually works perfectly on Hal's dad, yet has a little bit of an edge to it when Ryan wears it."

For Hal's car, Martin Campbell ordered up the muscle car he had seen in the 1971 cult classic film *Vanishing Point*: a 1970s Dodge Challenger. "That immediately gave a tone to the Hal Jordan character," says production designer Grant Major, who recalls choosing a color for the vehicle. "I've always liked the idea of giving him an orange car. For one, it stands out in a crowd, but orange is also complimentary to green, practically its opposite on the Munsell Color System. So it makes for a nice color transformation as well as character transformation, going from orange to green." As it turns out, Burnt Orange was popular in the '60s and '70s and was one of the Challenger's original colors. Subsequently, orange would become a color theme for Hal throughout the film; there are hints of it around his apartment and even on the F-35B he pilots.

Stage three at Second Line would become the home of Hal's apartment, but before that set was erected, Major and art director Iain McFadyen worked up a few concepts inspired by the modern, clean architectural designs common to Southern California beachside areas like Venice and Manhattan Beach. However, Campbell didn't want it to be too polished or sleek, instead preferring a more industrial style loft in the waterfront warehouse district. The final spacious design incorporates

huge bay windows overlooking Coast City; a matte painting would later be composited into these shots by visual effects.

Set decorator Anne Kuljian also wanted to steer clear of an upscale apartment, selecting an eclectic mix of metal and modern furniture, in addition to various personal objects Jordan would have collected over the years. "Hal makes a good living and can drop $7,000 on a sofa he likes or $10,000 on a bookcase, but he also has several found objects that are of interest to him, like an old lamp and chair from the original Ferris office; that chair and that lamp were in the office when he was a young boy. They're part of his life, just the way that his father is part of his life."

There was also a desire to give him a playful edge, Kuljian added. "We found this little remote control toy car, orange like his real car. We thought, wow, this is fun! So we put it on the coffee table, casually, like something he always had. I never thought it would be sharing the spotlight alongside the lantern itself."

Prior to filming, Major and Kuljian received the thumbs up from the man chosen to breathe life into Hal Jordan, actor Ryan Reynolds. Kuljian recalls the day Campbell and Reynolds came to rehearse on the set while she was still dressing. "Ryan came up to me and said, this is so perfect for the character. 'The set feels great! I love my loft!' So I knew that if he was happy there, if he was comfortable in the space, then it also meant that the movie would be better served."

Top: *This concept panorama of Coast City by Fabian Lacey was meant to represent the view from Hal Jordan's apartment.*

Above: *Hal Jordan's F-35B helmet by Paul Ozzimo.*

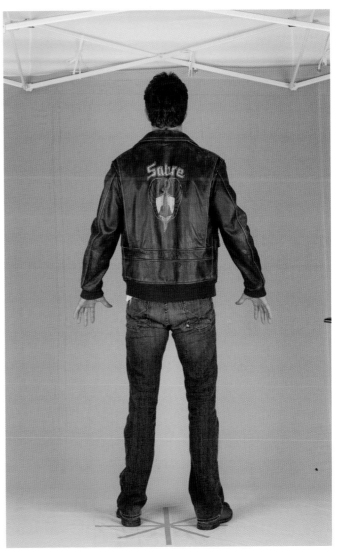

Left: *Hal Jordan's Dodge Challenger. Illustration by Tony Kieme. Hal Jordan by Simon Thorpe.*

Above: *Photography of actor Ryan Reynolds in costume as Hal Jordan used as reference for visual effects. Photos by Jim Berney.*

Constructing Green Lantern: From Page to Screen

Top left: *Hal Jordan's apartment. Photo by François Duhamel.*

Bottom left: *The Power Battery, also known as the lantern, sits on Hal's coffee table. Photo by François Duhamel.*

Right, top to bottom: *Filming in Hal's apartment on stage three at Second Line Stages. The visual effects team would later composite into the windows a panoramic view of Coast City. Photos by François Duhamel.*

ABIN SUR'S FINAL MISSION

Left: *Rodolfo Damaggio's final concept rendering of Abin's ship.*

Left, inset: *Director Martin Campbell sparked to this rendering by James Lima, which proposed a vertical ship for Abin Sur.*

Below: *Ngila Dickson's final costume design for Abin Sur. Art by Constantine Sekeris.*

Up on the big screen, audiences witness a massive, vertical spaceship slicing across the dark vastness of space. It heralds the appearance of the Green Lantern Abin Sur, protector of Space Sector 2814. On the page, however, the film's shooting script only specified the "massive" scale necessary for Abin's mission: to evacuate the inhabitants of a nearby galaxy. Director Martin Campbell workshopped the ship's designs with the conceptual team, but they were looking a bit too familiar, some even resembling *Star Trek* warships. Campbell envisioned a multipurpose transport vessel, with Abin standing at the helm, looking out at space through big bay windows.

Concept artist James Lima recalls being up late one night fiddling with the 3-D modeling program ZBrush when a polygon glitch caused him to sit up in his chair. "I was working on this organic alien creature, completely unrelated, and suddenly it contorted into this multi-angular shape. I spun the model around and thought, there's something here." Lima imported it into Photoshop for a quick paint over and brought it with him to the next meeting. Campbell immediately sparked to its verticality, but quizzed Lima on its purpose. Lima replied, "Why does every spaceship have to be horizontal like a submarine or a battleship? There is no up or down in space." The director was sold.

Production designer Grant Major recalls handing it off to concept artist Rodolfo Damaggio weeks later. "He buried himself in that job, deconstructing the original design and basically rebuilding it as a working piece of engineering. He did a fantastic job!" Damaggio's final 3-D Maya model of Abin's ship, based on Lima's concept, was then turned over to visual effects.

Campbell used the ship's verticality to great effect, designing a thrilling action sequence illustrated by storyboard artists Michael Anthony Jackson and Ray Harvie. Abin's clash with the terrifying entity Parallax plays out over the ship's multiple levels and leaves Abin mortally wounded and rushing down to the escape pod at the base of the vessel. Although the sequence was trimmed substantially to accommodate story revisions, the essence of it remains, and Abin barely escapes the battle.

Top: *Michele Moen's cosmic painting depicting one of the film's opening sequences incorporates Rodolfo Damaggio's 3-D model of Abin Sur's ship.*

Above: *Interior of Abin's ship by Rodolfo Damaggio.*

Right: *Early study of Abin's ship interior by Alex Laurant.*

WINDOWS

NAVIGATION
CONTROLS

HANU'S CASKET

CARGO / STORAGE

WINDOWS

CENTRAL
PROPULSION
CORE &
ENGINE

ESCAPE POD

ABIN
SUR'S
SHIP

ROUGH CROSS-SECTION

Right: *Rodolfo Damaggio modeled and textured Abin Sur's ship in 3-D.*

Below: *Spherical controls for the ship by Fabian Lacey.*

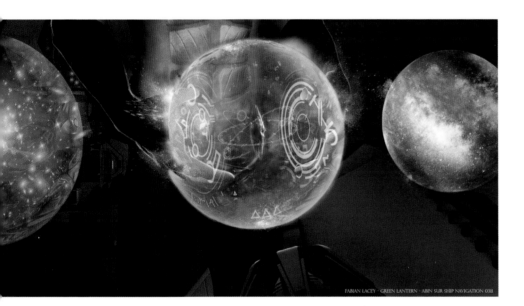

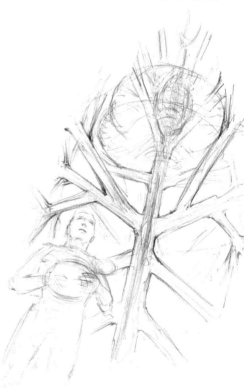

"Martin wanted the escape pod to be small and confined," recalls Major. "I thought, a person who's in pain immediately scrunches up into a fetal position. It's an existential thing, really, just you and your pain. The image that struck me was Leonardo da Vinci's fetus in the womb." Major produced a few sketches, working with concept artist Ed Natividad, and then Paul Ozzimo, who refined the design in 3-D. A protective clamshell was added around the sphere to protect it from the elements and deliver Abin safely to Earth.

Abin's fateful encounter with Hal Jordan was shot on location in Madisonville, Louisiana, with a meticulously built full-scale version of the escape pod that was partially submerged in water. The pivotal scene culminates in a gripping moment when the mortally wounded spaceman opens his hand and reveals the Power Ring. "It chose you," he tells Jordan. Abin then turns his head toward his lantern, wincing in pain, "Place the ring, speak the oath . . . " With his last breath, Abin imparts his duties and responsibilities as protector of Space Sector 2814 to the first human ever chosen: Hal Jordan, who has absolutely no idea what any of this means.

Above: *Pencil sketch by Grant Major of Abin's ship interior.*

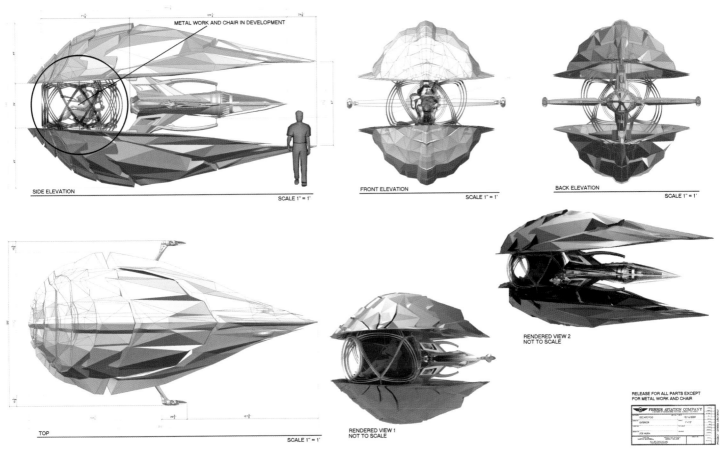

Top: *Abin's escape pod jettisons from the mother ship. Rendering by Fabian Lacey, revisions by Paul Christopher.*

Above: *Construction drawings for Abin's escape pod by Joe Hiura and Paul Ozzimo.*

His ring 'constructs' a hologram of Sinestro.

SINESTRO: "Your mission to evacuate them... is no longer necessary. It is just as it was on Talok. Every life form destroyed; their essence... absorbed."

ABIN: "And the Guardians?"
*NOTE: The yellow flare is slightly stronger behind him.

ABIN: "Sinestro. I'm traveling at maximum velocity: Tell Fentara I should reach his sector by --

SINESTRO: "The Guardians are silent."
*NOTE: The sound of his voice and the image fizzle out. ALSO, The yellow flare is across Abin's back.

SINESTRO: "Fentara is dead."

He turns and steps forward --
*NOTE: The yellow flare is reflected on his face.

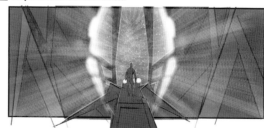

-- moving towards the window (flaring yellow around the edges).

ABIN: "But the planet's inhabiants -- "
*NOTE: A slight yellow flaring behind Abin.

A sudden piercing scream, as thousands of shrieking faces (Parallax) slam against the window --

This spread: *Storyboard excerpts, ABIN VS PARALLAX sequence (Scenes 13-15 / Shots 80-220 / April 14, 2010). Storyboard artist: Ray Harvie.*

-- imploding it. Abin is hurled backwards.

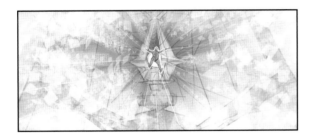

He ricochets off some infrastructure, drops past lens.

CAMERA TRACKS WITH HIM as he plunges down.
*NOTE: Because the window has been broken, some loose objects in the ship will be sucked up and past lens.

He bounces off a metal platform.

CAMERA TRACKS BACK with him as he regains control. The dark monster is like an avalanche behind him.

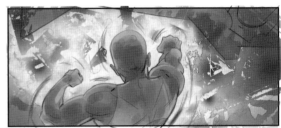

He turns --

-- and fires a green energy blast from his ring.

-- that hits Parallax as he begins to envelop the lens from behind.

YELLOW ENERGY
ATTACKING ABIN SUR
STAGE 3

ABIN-SUR DEATH TRANSFORMATION 01

Above: *Parallax attacks Abin Sur in this key frame by Seth Engstrom.*

Left: *Proposal showing how Abin's Green Lantern suit could dissolve at the time of his death. Art by Constantine Sekeris.*

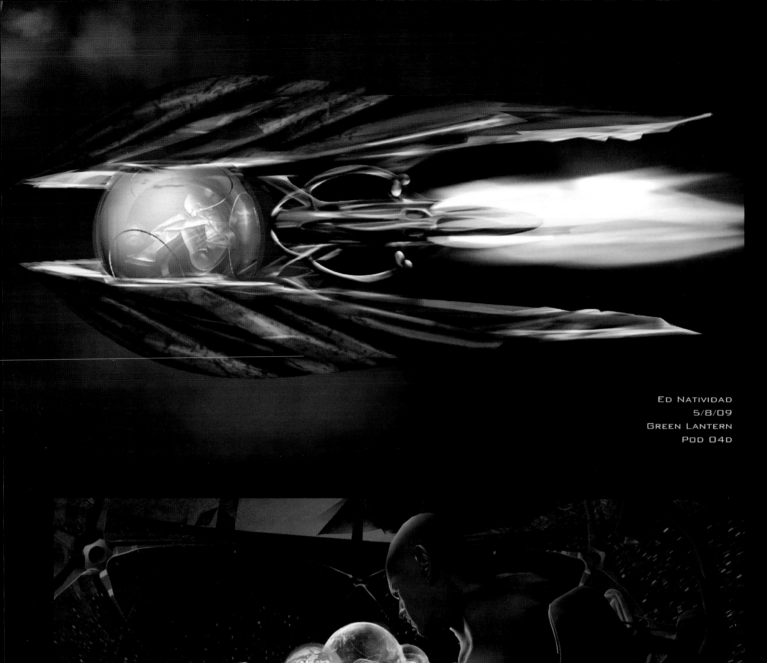

ED NATIVIDAD
5/8/09
GREEN LANTERN
POD 04D

ABIN SUR ESCAPE POD · NAVIGATION · FABIAN LACEY

Top: *Early escape pod concept by Ed Natividad.*

Above: *Inside the escape pod, the mortally wounded Abin Sur searches for*

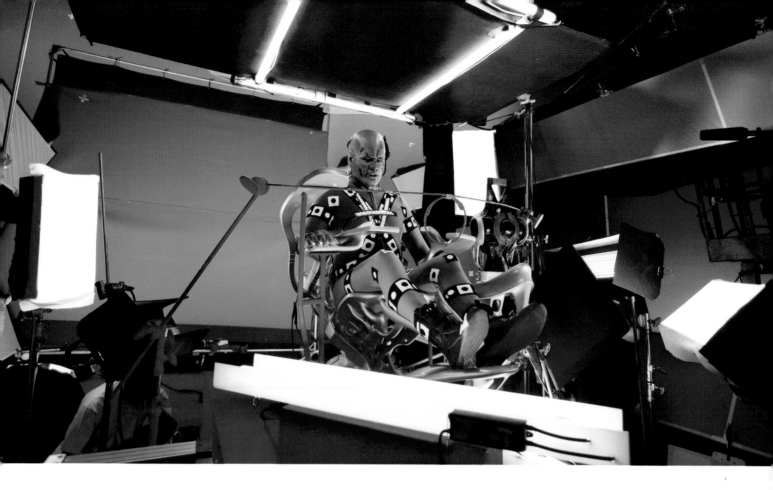

Top: *Actor Temuera Morrison in full makeup as Abin Sur, films scenes in the escape pod. For shots requiring the pod and its components to be added in digitally, non-occlusional set pieces were added for eyeline and camera framing. In this case, the navigation controls were indicated. The surrounding environment and Abin's Green Lantern uniform would also be added by the visual effects team in post-production. Photo by François Duhamel.*

Above: *Paul Ozzimo's final concept illustration of Abin's escape pod.*

Left: *Modelmaker Brett Phillips built various study models during the pre-production phase. Photo by Brett Phillips.*

Right: *The stage is set, and cameras stand by to capture the perfect sunset. Photo by Rosa Palomo.*

Above: *Paul Ozzimo based this concept illustration of the crash site on a photo of the shooting location.*

Right: *Pencil study by Grant Major.*

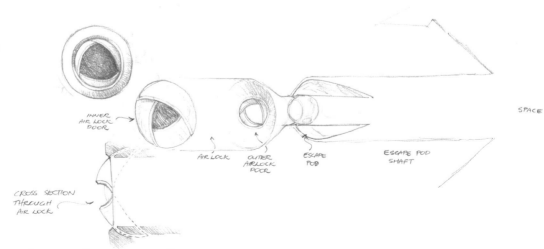

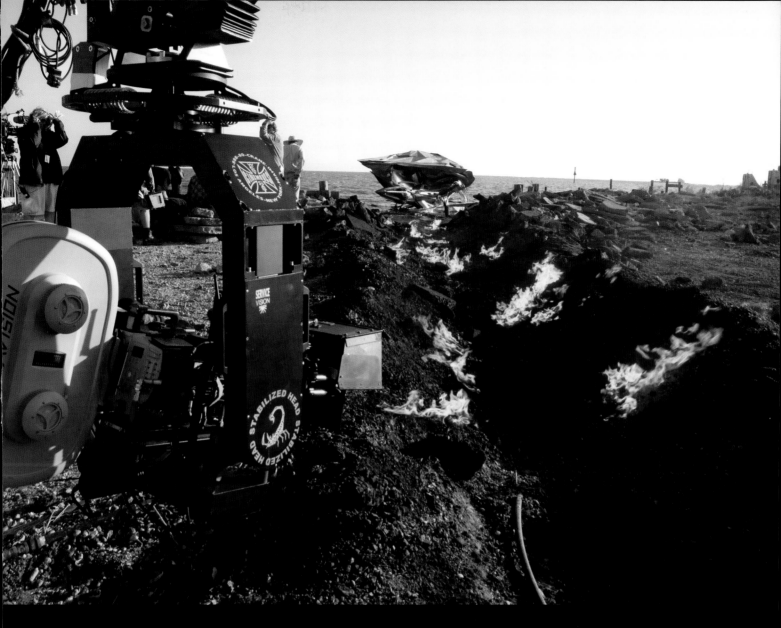

Left: *Divers prep the crashed pod on location near New Orleans. Photo by Rosa Palomo.*

Above: *Abin's pod is lowered into the water. Right to left: Grant Major, Martin Campbell, and Gary Powell. Photo by*

Above: *The prosthetic makeup effects department, headed by Joel Harlow, created this full-scale, lifelike body of Abin Sur. The body played a pivotal role in front of the cameras, but it was also scanned and meticulously photographed for use by the visual effect team for creating Abin's digital double. Photo by Leah Hardstark.*

Right: *Temuera Morrison in full Abin Sur makeup. Photo courtesy Joel Harlow.*

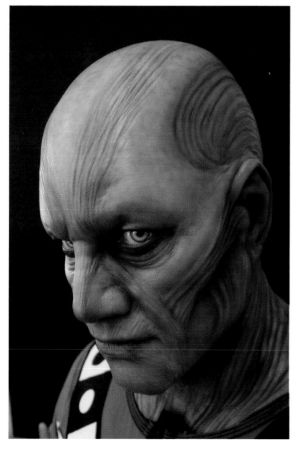

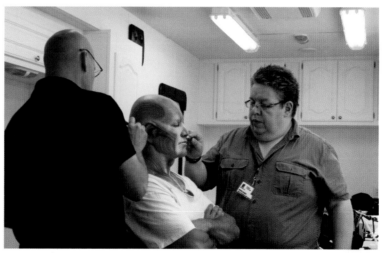

Top: *Richie Alonzo sculpts Abin's visage, while the alien body takes shape in the mirror's reflection. Photo courtesy Joel Harlow.*

Above: *Richie Alonzo (right) and David Dupuis apply the Abin makeup to actor Temuera Morrison. The prosthetics team had to devise a unique painting system to achieve the character's high chroma, violet skin tone. "There was nothing available cosmetically off-the-shelf that approached that color," explains Alonzo. The multiple facial appliances were pre-painted then blended together, covering Morrison's entire head, all the way up to his lashes. Stunning blue lenses completed the look. Photo courtesy Joel Harlow.*

PART II

ICUICU : צוכ|כ|ט

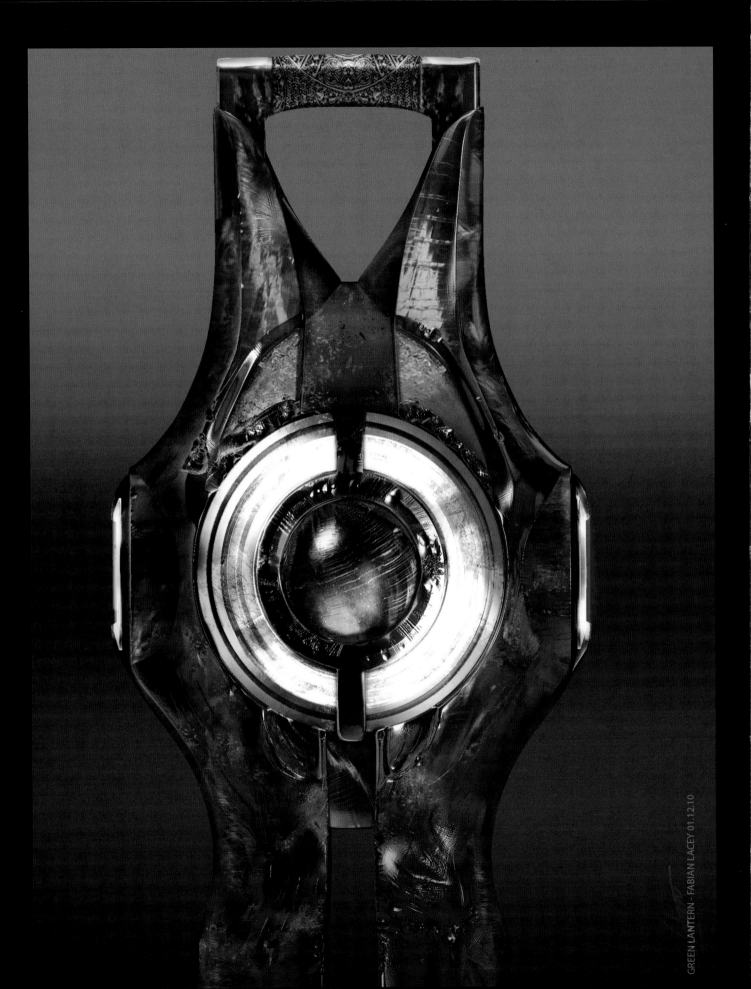

THE LANTERN, THE RING, AND THE JOURNEY

Left: *Final design for the Power Battery by Fabian Lacey.*

Below: *This concept by Christopher Ross stood as the approved Power Battery for months, but its design was subsequently altered to tie into the overall look of Planet Oa.*

The Green Lantern's Power Battery—commonly referred to as the lantern—and his Power Ring are considered to be among the most instantly recognizable items in the pantheon of American comic books. Although the origin of the Power Battery was updated as part of the comic's Silver Age reimagining, its design retains the look of a vintage railroad lantern from the comic's original Golden Age debut. In contrast, various comic book artists have altered and updated the design of the Power Ring throughout the years. To adapt these iconic pieces faithfully for cinema, it was essential for the filmmakers to have a full understanding of their history and function within the context of the story.

Billions of years ago, at the very center of the universe, on a barren planet called Oa, the immortal Guardians of the Universe set out to create an interstellar police force that would help bring order to the universe. The Guardians harnessed the collective willpower of the universe, in the form of Green Energy, within a massive reactor known as the Central Power Battery. They then forged individual Power Rings and portable Power Batteries (lanterns) for each member of the Green Lantern Corps. When a Power Ring's energy is depleted, the Green Lanterns use their Power Battery as a remote charging station.

Initial designs for the film version of the Power Battery, rendered by concept designer Christopher Ross, were much more derivative of the comics. At production designer Grant Major's request, Ross incorporated a Fresnel lens (commonly found in old lighthouses) motif into its architecture, but the overall color, shape, and texture still conveyed a vintage metallic railroad lantern. Director Martin Campbell and producer Donald De Line approved the design, and for more than eight months of pre-production it was considered final. However, Ross's Power Battery design does not appear in the final film.

Just prior to principal photography, Drew Petrotta, the film's property master, requested the final Power Battery design so that he could begin fabricating them. Before turning it over, supervising art director François Audouy asked concept designer Fabian Lacey to adjust a few details on Ross's initial design to better capture the look of Planet Oa. Although Lacey liked the Power Battery's iconic lantern shape from the comics, he felt its origin required it to look foreign and alien. It needed to have a sense of mystery and history, all while maintaining its function. With that in mind, he decided to veer off the current design path. "Basically, I took a leap of faith and went in a completely different direction, just to see where it would lead me." Lacey pitched Major the concept: "It all comes from the Guardians. The Central Battery, the Power Battery, and the Power Ring all work together and should therefore share certain properties. Besides the Fresnel-looking lens, it should also share the dark glassy-quartz materiality of the indigenous Oan rock that houses the Central Battery. Maybe that's the only material in the universe that can contain that kind of power," Lacey rationalized. He also added an engraved inscription around the handle. "It's something personalized, belonging to the Green Lantern Corps. This Power Battery is an honorable, ancient power source that has been passed down from one Green Lantern to another for millions and millions of years."

The design was well received by Major, who anxiously said at the time, "Now, let's see what Martin and Donald think." Lacey explains, "It was a little risky because it's such an important piece, and it was so different from what we had all discussed doing for such a long time. We didn't know how they would react."

Lacey recalls the day his illustration was pinned up on the wall, among many other designs up for review that day. "Martin came into the room and immediately walked straight up to the Power Battery and said, 'What the *bleep* is that?!'" Campbell was instantly drawn to it. "It was the right middle ground between recognizable and unearthly exotic," adds Major. The director immediately recognized it as the Power Battery, but there was a new flavor connecting it to Oa, which De Line also liked. Campbell exclaimed, "Let's do it. Let's go all the way." Lacey found out later that it had also received the blessing of Green Lantern comic book writer and DC Comics Chief Creative Officer, Geoff Johns. Lacey says, "That was definitely the most satisfying, because I had set out to capture the spirit of the Power Battery from the comics."

With the schedule closing in, Lacey was given two weeks to turn his illustration into a final 3-D digital sculpture. He modeled the Power Battery in ZBrush and finally turned it over to property master Drew Petrotta, who with Lewis Doty at Studio Art & Technology in Sunland, California, produced five prototypes of varying shapes and sizes. "They're grown in a rapid prototyping machine, which uses lasers in a resin vat to cut out the shapes from Fabian's digital model," explains Petrotta. Once the design and size were approved, one final piece was produced, which they molded and cast with a green-tinted resin. Multiples were eventually made for the film, each one hollowed out and hand carved internally to create the material's inner fissures and grooves.

The Power Battery then underwent various lighting and camera tests, supervised by cinematographer Dion Beebe. Beebe and chief lighting technician John Buckley, along with Petrotta and painter Tony Leonardi, experimented with light and paint to achieve a perfect combination that brought it to life.

As a consequence of the Power Battery's successful redesign, Major sought to revisit the Power Ring and incorporate the same Oan motifs into its design. Concept designer Joe Hiura had noticed that the Power Ring concepts weren't resonating with Major or Campbell, and although he was busy on another assignment, Hiura asked Audouy if he could take a crack at it. "I actually volunteered to do it on my own time. I had designed jewelry in the past and felt I could bring something to the table. Also, it was a great

Left, from top: *A sample of digital renderings show the evolving design of Green Lantern's Power Ring:*
1. Preliminary concept by Christopher Ross.
2, 2a. Simplified "collegiate" concept by Joe Hiura.
3, 3a. Ngila Dickson and Grant Major worked closely with Hiura to generate this final design, incorporating the iconic Green Lantern symbol and Oan design motifs.

LANTERN ENERGY
THE INTERIOR IMPERFECTIONS IN THE STONE, ILLUMINATE, CREATING AN ALIEN TEXT.

THE LIGHT INSIDE MOVES IN A CIRCULAR MOTION, REVEALING TEXT AS IT PASSES.

GLOWING ROCK EXAMPLES

GREEN ENERGY
RING CHARGE v001

ENERGY: AS THE RING GETS CLOSE TO THE LANTERN, THE LANTERN GLOWS BRIGHTER ILLUMINATING THE FRACTURES INSIDE THE STONE. WHEN THE RING GET TO A CERTIAN DISTANCE, A PLASMA CONTACT IS MADE. PLASMA SHOOTS OUT FROM THE RING, AND THE LANTERN, MEETING IN THE MIDDLE.

Top: *Seth Engstrom's concept for the illuminated Power Battery also proposed revealing an alien text within the surface of the Battery as a way to unveil the Green Lantern Oath to Hal Jordan.*

Above: *One of Engstrom's more powerful concept illustrations depicts the Green Energy roiling out of the Power Battery and charging the Ring.*

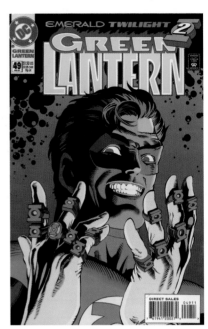

Top Left: *Taika Waititi (left), who plays Hal's best friend Tom Kalmaku, observes cinematographer Dion Beebe prep the Power Battery prop. "Dion would treat it like a commercial product shot," says property master Drew Petrotta. Photo by François Duhamel.*

Top Right: *Cover of* Green Lantern *no. 49 (February 1994). Art by Daryl Banks and Romeo Tanghal.*

Above: *Variations on a theme by Fabian Lacey.*

Right: *Screen grab of Lacey's 3-D model of the Power Battery.*

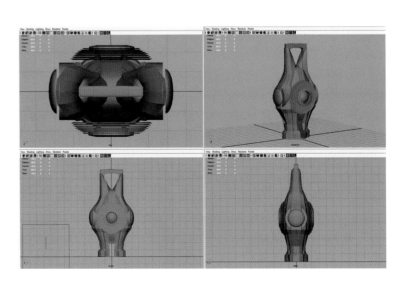

Above: *Hal Jordan prepares to make contact. Photo by François Duhamel.*

Pages 76–77: *Storyboard excerpts, FIRST FLIGHT sequence (Scene 59, Shots 10-40 / Scene 60, Shots 10-40 / Scene 61, Shots 10-20 / October 23, 2009). Storyboard artist: Michael Anthony Jackson.*

Page 77, bottom right: *Hal travels through the wormhole. Concept illustration by Michele Moen.*

opportunity to do a ring for Grant, who helped design the most famous, precious ring to rule them all," Hiura quips.

Initially, Major and Campbell wanted to explore a subtle design, concerned that if the Power Ring were too flashy or obvious, a distracted audience would begin to wonder why all those around Hal Jordan weren't asking questions. Hiura did approximately a half dozen variations of a similarly themed design, from which one was approved. Much more restrained than anything in the comics, it was shaped more like a junior collegiate ring, and the typical Green Lantern symbol was substituted with the Fresnel lens design. Prototypes were grown and shipped to New Orleans, but upon inspection, costume designer Ngila Dickson became concerned that the Power Ring's design was too restrained, too delicate, and that it needed to preserve the iconic Green Lantern symbol. She was able to persuade Campbell to allow her and Major to revisit the design.

Dickson and Major found inspiration right outside the soundstage on actor Ryan Reynolds's hand; a ring he himself was wearing at the time. They liked the thickness and solidity of it, but most of all they liked the way it fit him. Subsequent collaborations with Dickson, Major and Hiura, who modeled the Power Ring using the 3-D program SolidWorks, yielded the final design that was sent to Sunland. Forty-eight hours later, the final Ring arrived in New Orleans, with multiples following soon afterward. As with the Power Battery, the ring's final finish relied on Dion Beebe, says Petrotta. "These pieces look as good as they do on film because whenever we shot inserts, Dion would treat it like a commercial product shot. He took great care and detail lighting them."

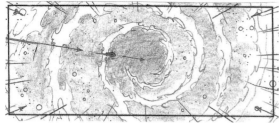

See Hal enter the shot.

CAMERA FLIES BACK with Hal.

Hal in flight - the Ring firing ahead to...

...rip opena massive swirling DARK CIRCLE IN SPACE - A WORMHOLE.
(CAMERA CHASING HAL)

Hal is pulled into it.

Hal tries to veer, but the Ring has taken over, the green comet of Hal flies straight.
CAMERA FLIES BACK with Hal gaining.

Into the wormhole's center.

Wormhole closes up behind Hal in a burst of light. HAL ENVELOPED IN BLACK.

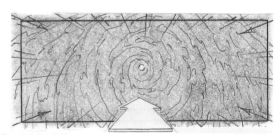

Overwhelming. Endless.
(HAL'S POV FLYING THRU BLACK/WORMHOLE)

Hal sailing through it -- no light at the end of this tunnel -- until...
CAMERA FLIES BACK WITH HAL.

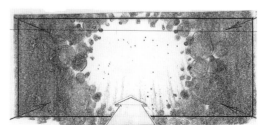

Green creeps in. Just enough to hint at an end in sight-- then building-- growing--
HAL'S POV FLYING THRU BLACK/WORMHOLE CONT.

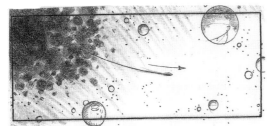

See Hal exit the wormhole...

...until the Green Light envelopes Hal.
CAMERA FLIES BACK WITH HAL.

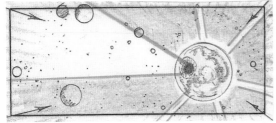

Just a glimpse of it's source... a resplendent aquamarine planet lit by four suns. Oa.
CAMERA FLIES TOWARDS OA.

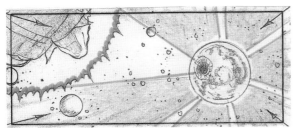

Hal enters frame.

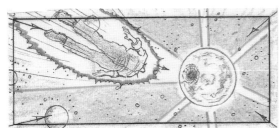

...Flying towards Oa.

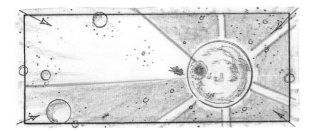

CAMERA FLIES BACK WITH HAL.

CAMERA FLIES BACK WITH HAL GAINING.

FADE OUT TO GREEN.

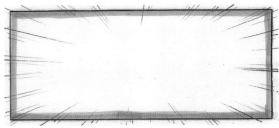

A rush of voices, soft at first, then overlapping, insistent.

THROUGH THE WORMHOLE AND INTO UNIFORM

Left: *Hal leaves Coast City behind as he's rocketed into space. Concept illustration by Rodolfo Damaggio.*

Summoned to the planet Oa for his induction and training, the unsuspecting Hal Jordan is rocketed through the cosmos and into a colossal swirling wormhole, courtesy of his new Power Ring. Emerging through the ominous space tunnel, he catches a glimpse of the resplendent planet just before drifting into one of the massive beams of Green Energy and drifting out of consciousness.

The tailored green and black suit Jordan wakes up in is not made of fabric, or rubber, or anything recognizable from our physical world. And it's formfitting—extremely formfitting. Generated by the Power Ring's Green Energy, the uniform is essentially a construct of solid light that has been grafted onto Hal's DNA. For costume designer Ngila Dickson, who does not own a Power Ring and has spent her career working in our physical world (and in J. R. R. Tolkien's Middle Earth), designing the Green Lantern costume proved challenging. She does, however, possess a lot of willpower—huge amounts of it. "I love the idea of tackling things that stretch and test me, and I love working with my old mate Grant Major," she says. "Films are becoming a balancing act between digitally driven projects and physically driven projects, but I'm still a costume designer. I bring to visual effects an understanding about fabrics, about shapes, about how things fit the human body, about detail."

Dickson studied the DC comic book series, from John Broome to Geoff Johns, tracking the evolution of Hal Jordan's Green Lantern suit over the years. And she made a startling discovery: it hasn't changed much. "I'm always very conscious of the fan base for these sorts of characters. You don't want to wander too far away, but you do want to absolutely push every boundary you possibly can," she says. Dickson's design for the suit developed out of its functionality and purpose. That meant thinking like a Guardian. "I needed to get into their big blue heads," she jests. "We set up this notion of DNA being the basis of everyone's costume. This process occurs as part of every Green Lantern's induction. The Guardians inspect the DNA of every creature, wherever they come from, and then they go for

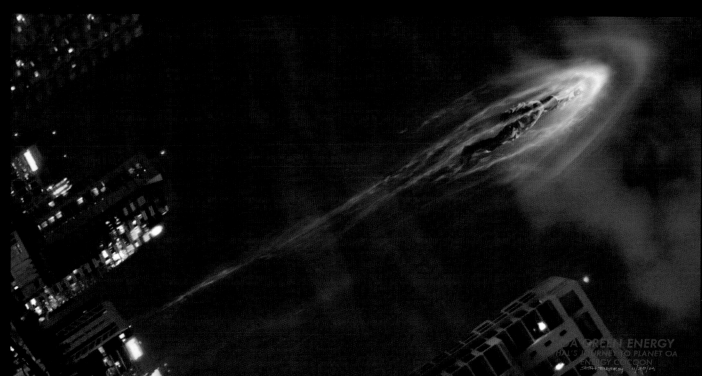

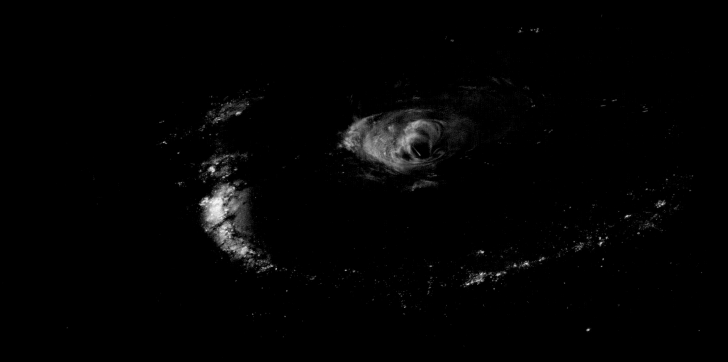

Left: *Green Energy from the Power Ring envelops the unsuspecting test pilot. Concept illustration by Seth Engstrom.*

Below: *Engstrom's concept for the energy cocoon that transports Hal Jordan into the unknown.*

Bottom: *Into the wormhole. Concept illustration by Michele Moen.*

perfecting the body," explains Dickson. Aware that Jordan needs a disguise element on Earth, they also give him a mask.

That concept became the launching point for each suit, which meant that every single member of the Green Lantern Corps would have an individual style. Using the green and black vernacular and the Green Lantern symbol, Dickson designed each costume to be unique to each wearer. "I've been fortunate enough to find myself working with two artists who really kind of get me. I think that's always the key to making things like this work the way you want them to," she says, praising illustrators Simon Thorpe and Constantine Sekeris.

The human body is the architectural foundation for Hal Jordan's Green Lantern suit, so for inspiration, Dickson turned to the father of modern human anatomy, sixteenth century Dutch anatomist Andreas Vesalius and his collection of illustrative works, *De Humani Corporis Fabrica* (*On the Workings of the Human Body*). She also observed marine creatures like the tuna, and even chartered a field trip to Sea World in San Diego to examine a dolphin's skin texture up close. Working through all these references, in addition to cars, planes, and aerospace designs, were an essential part of the development process. "Hal Jordan is a fighter pilot by nature, and I wanted to combine this super skin with a very aerodynamic design," explains Dickson. The mask was also purely about function, she says. "In the design we even added a change to the bone structure around Reynolds' eyes to help enhance the disguise; the Guardians would have. His eyes also turn gossamer, as in the comics."

The choice to make the Green Lantern suits entirely digital was not made arbitrarily. Multiple factors contributed to the final decision, none more than cost and feasibility. Dickson elaborates: "It never occurred to me for a moment that we would be doing this as a purely digital costume. It was a real nerve-racking choice, but in fact, all that does is drive me to make it great. I'm a very detailed, realistic designer. So this was the challenge for this one, making it real." The technical process, she says, is not that dissimilar to actually making something with fabric. "I know in my head what I ultimately want to see and feel, and my hope is that what audiences see on screen will be as tactile as a piece of clothing."

In terms of the digital design, the suit consists of three layers: an underlayer, an overlayer, and the Green Energy. "There's a whole life force underneath it that is attached to the human body. Over that, there's an aerodynamic cellular skin texture. Then the third element is the Green Energy from the Power Ring, which brings it all to life. When you see those three elements together to form the Green Lantern suit, that's when it gets really interesting visually," she says.

For filming, gray spandex tracking suits dotted with fixed black and white markers were worn by actors Ryan Reynolds, Temuera Morrison, who plays Hal's predecessor Abin Sur, and Mark Strong, who portrays Hal Jordan's austere mentor Thaal Sinestro. The selected film footage from the main cameras, and from two "witness" cameras nearby, would be sent off to resolve the suit's positions in three-dimensional space. Using proprietary computer software, they were able to triangulate each fixed point within the frame and figure out the exact position of each joint on the actor's body. Sony Pictures Imageworks then applied that data to the 3-D digital skeletons of the characters, essentially locking the digital suit element to the live-action film footage of the actor's body, which in turn served as a guide to drive the animation.

Above: *The Power Ring whisks Hal Jordan to Planet Oa.*

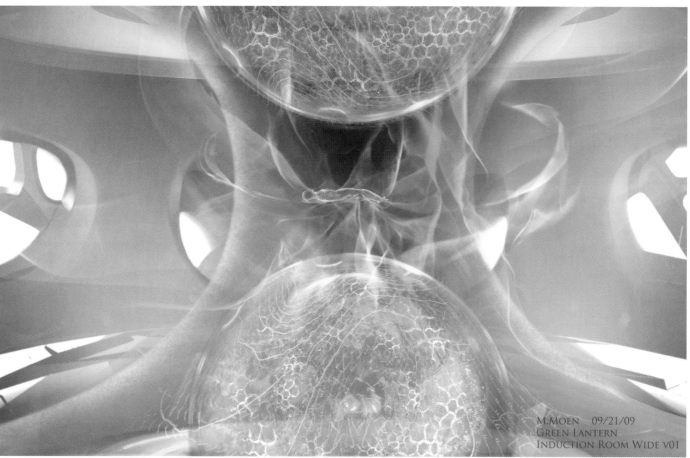

Top: *Hal Jordan's induction on Oa. Concept illustration by James Lima. Revisions by Rodolfo Damaggio.*

Above: *Induction room concept illustration by Michele Moen.*

I.MOEN 09/09/09
RFEN LANTERN
AN WAKE-UP ROOM_V02

Left: *Hal regains consciousness in a non-descript room, already wearing the Green Lantern uniform. While the inside of the Oan wakeup room (above) was inspired by the interior pearlescent enamel of a seashell, the textured patina for the exterior of the building (below) was based on reference images of ancient Roman glass from the Getty Villa museum in Malibu, California. Grant Major wanted the iridescence to be partially covered by patterned crust-like impurities, implying millions of years of "Oan pollution, which give the structure a more real, older feel." Concept illustrations by Michele Moen. Early Green Lantern costume concept by E.J. Krisor.*

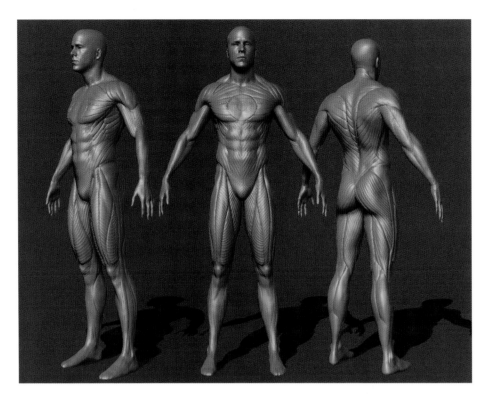

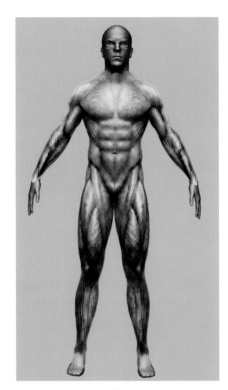

Top left: *3-D model of the suit modeled on a scan of actor Ryan Reynolds. Artist: Simon Thorpe.*

Top right: *The muscle underlayer of the suit by Constantine Sekeris.*

Right: *Colored 3-D rendering by Simon Thorpe.*

Opposite top and bottom: *Ngila Dickson drew inspiration for the suit's line patterns from the father of modern human anatomy, Andreas Vesalius. Art by Simon Thorpe.*

Opposite right: *One of Dickson's first concepts for the Green Lantern suit incorporated the comic book character's famous white gloves, but through the course of development the filmmakers realized that their were certain aspects of the comics that wouldn't translate well to the live-action film. Art by Simon Thorpe.*

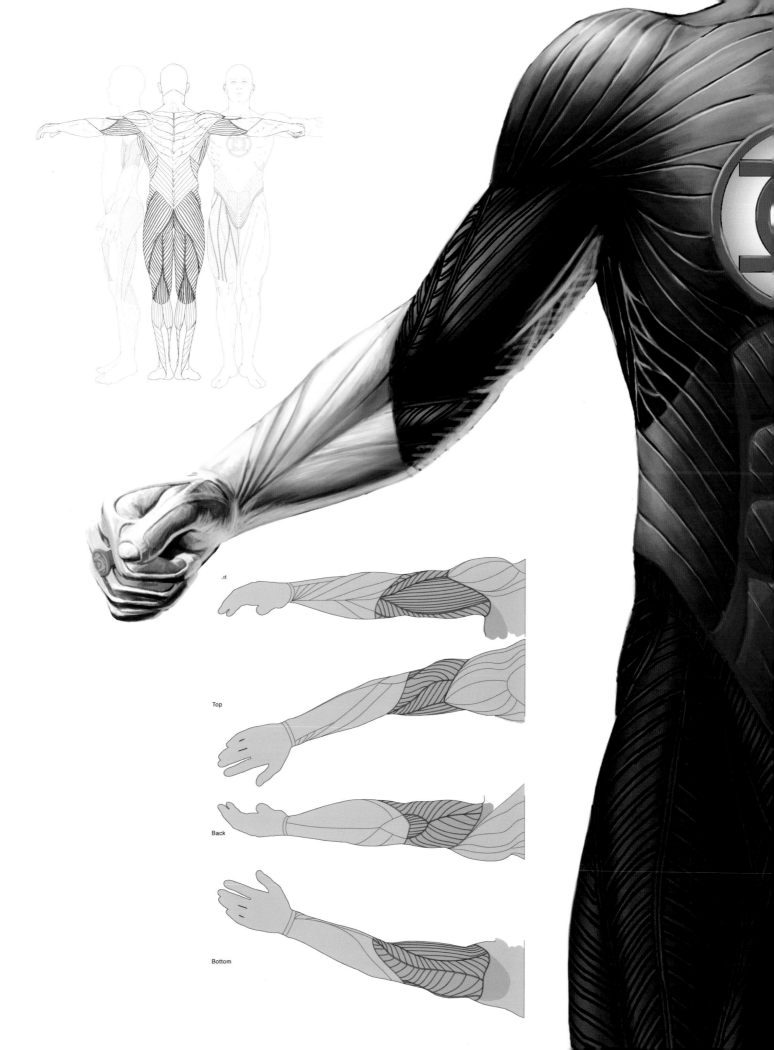

.t

Top

Back

Bottom

Constructing Green Lantern: From Page to Screen

Left: *Penultimate costume concept. Illustration by Constantine Sekeris.*

Right: *Ngila Dickson's final design of the Green Lantern suit. Illustration by Constantine Sekeris.*

He looks around, disoriented, confused, scared. He notices: He's wearing the Lantern uniform.

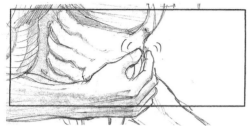

He pulls at it, trying to take it off. But it's part of his skin. What the hell?

He tries to find a way out, but there's no exit. Breathing hard now, he tries to get control of himself. LOW ANGLE MCS HAL looks camera left.

Then he looks down at his uniform again. It is very, very cool. Fascinated, he studies it.

Hal takes a turn, checking out the back of the uniform. Hal admires himself in the mirror... flexes.

Then holds out his arms. Is this me? Am I dreaming?

MCS Hal smiles to himself... turns... exits camera right.

But no, it seems real. Maybe another turn, a pose or two. CAMERA PAN RIGHT with Hal.

Hal turns, moves camera left.

CAMERA PANS LEFT with Hal... See Tomar-Re in F.G.

VOICE (O.S.): Are you quite finished? PAN LEFT ENDS. Hal turns to see...

A fin-headed, bird-beaked fish-man in a similar Green Lantern uniform. TOMAR-RE. With him is the formidable figure of SINESTRO.

Left: *Storyboard excerpts,
WAKE-UP ROOM sequence
(Scene 67 / Shots 2-10 /
December 10, 2009).
Storyboard artist: Michael
Anthony Jackson.*

Right: *Final shots, as they
appear in the film.*

PLANET OA

Left: *Vertical panorama of the 'Sacre Coeur,' the focal point of the city and entrance to the Central Battery. Final concept illustration by Michele Moen.*

Below: *An example of Oan architecture by Rodolfo Damaggio. It was dubbed "Donald's Carbon Building" after producer Donald De Line.*

For countless millennia, the Guardians of the Universe have called Planet Oa their home, and it is also the headquarters of the Green Lantern Corps. Director Martin Campbell and production designer Grant Major wanted to create a place unlike anything audiences had seen before, and they had about two years to do it. "It took months of kicking around ideas and researching natural and architectural references," recalls Major, who wanted to imbue the city with a multilayered, complex historical texture.

"Grant wanted some of the architecture to be so ancient that it would be impossible to distinguish it from the landscape," recalls concept artist Justin Sweet. Almost every artist did a version of what the city would look like, but Sweet's interpretation was the first to capture the majesty, grandeur, and mystery that Campbell and Major were after. "My process is completely emotional. I've got to transport myself when I work, and this was simply my emotional take on what Oa felt like to me and what I wanted to see while I was flying around with my lantern," says Sweet. His fantastical renderings soon became a visual palette for the city, but the process to actualize his painterly concepts without diminishing their spectacle would require more work. "You begin with these extraordinary ideas, and then you have to keep developing them and working on them until they become real," adds Major.

A large part of the challenge was conceiving a unique architectural language for each of the city's structures. Major wanted them not only to be varied in time, from the more ancient to the more recent, but he also wanted them to be distinctly unique from one another, reflecting the multiple styles and functions of the various alien species inhabiting them. "It definitely took a while, and many artists," says concept artist Rodolfo Damaggio. "Designing these structures for aliens meant that we had to avoid terrestrial features such as doors, windows, and columns, yet they still needed to be grounded in their own logic for it to be realistic," he says. These key architectural buildings, many of which Damaggio designed, were then named for tracking purposes. For example, "Donald's Carbon Building" was named after producer Donald De Line because it was his favorite.

GREEN LANTERN
JUSTIN 2009 M.MOEN 07/27/10
WIDE OA PLANET SALUTE WIP1

GREEN LANTERN
MMOEN · 082010

Top: *Beams of energy from the Green Lantern Corp's salute shoot through the planet's porous surface in this wide overview of Oa by Justin*

Above: *A hazy atmosphere shrouds the Oan city in mystery. Concept illustration by Michele Moen.*

Top: *Oan landscape and color palette studies by Justin Sweet.*

Above: *This early conceptual illustration by Justin Sweet was the first to capture the majesty, grandeur, and mystery the filmmakers wanted for Oa.*

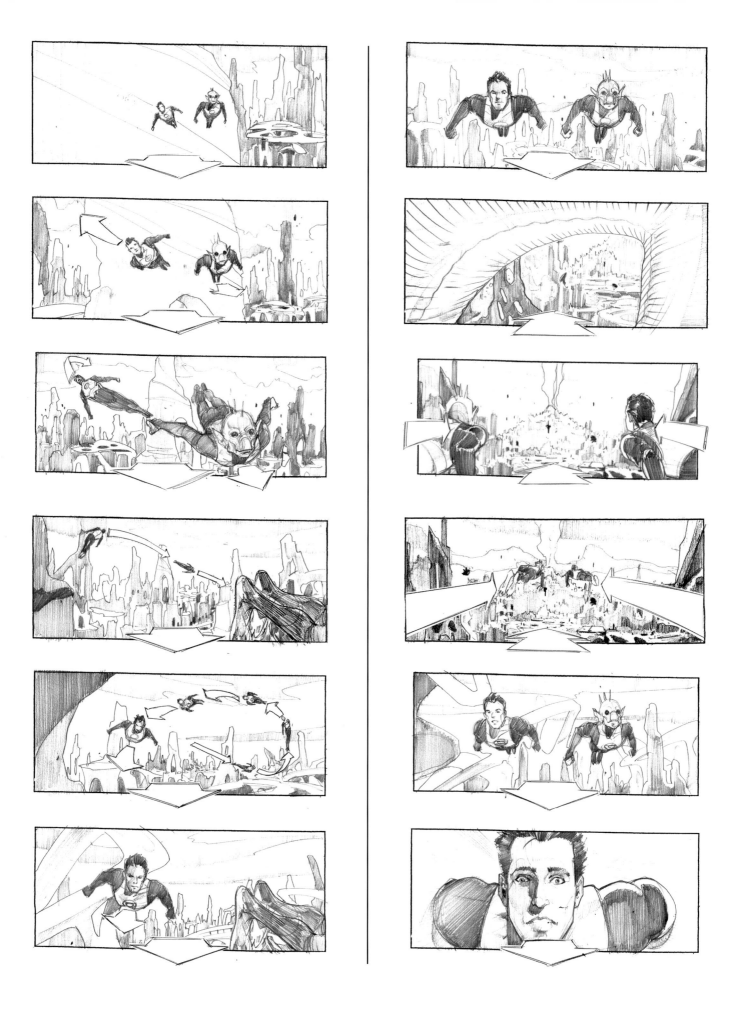

Left: *These storyboard panels of the GREAT LEAP sequence in which Tomar-Re leads Hal Jordan on a tour of Oa, complimented the pre-visualization team's animated version of the sequence and Michele Moen's key frame illustrations. All these elements, along with filmed footage of actor Ryan Reynolds were then assembled and inserted into the working cut of the film by editor Stuart Baird, months before any proper visual effects shots were delivered. Storyboard artist: Collin Grant.*

Above: *Early conceptual illustrations by Justin Sweet.*

Michele Moen rendered multiple key frames depicting specific camera angles from the GREAT LEAP sequence.

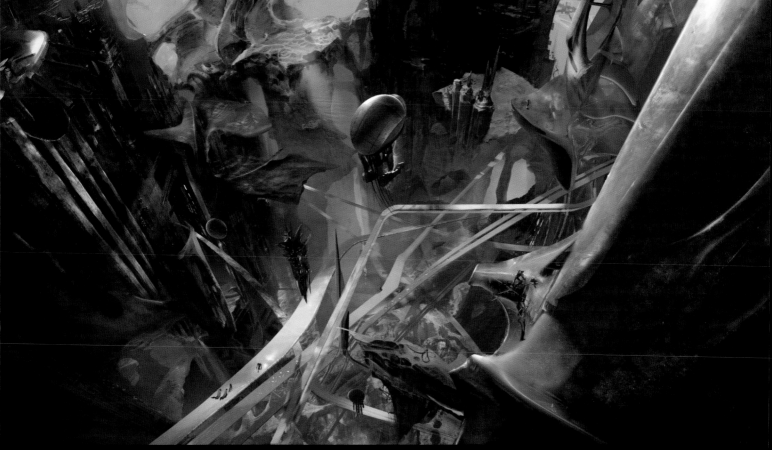

While these buildings helped establish an architectural language for the city, it was concept artist and noted matte painter Michele Moen who merged them with Sweet's work, translating his painterly conceptual renderings into final photographic appearances. Moen's paintings were considered to be the finished look, and served as locked-down, specific reference frames for the visual effects team to build their fully digital Oan environments.

Moen's traditional matte paintings can be seen in films such as *Blade Runner* (1982), *Ghostbusters* (1984), and *Dick Tracy* (1990), but she says that she's now fully immersed in the digital realm. "As much as I would love to paint a matte shot in oils again, there are many more possibilities in digitally painting a jaw dropping, unbelievably real scene. Ultimately, no matter how it is accomplished, it must tell the story." And Moen's storytelling can be seen in the pearlescent light that is constantly bouncing and changing throughout Oa's atmosphere, and in the iridescent mists that give the city a magical yet moody quality.

In addition to the architectural structures from Sweet and Damaggio, Moen also had to create additional elements to populate the entire city. "The very first step to composing a painting is to lay in bold shapes that tell the story and read well graphically. Once that composition is locked, I'll paint the structures, landscapes, and environmental elements on individual layers in Photoshop. Because Oa is very sculptural and textural, I used reference from microscopic and macro nature photography: sea shells, coral, butterfly wings, tropical bird feathers, insect eyes, water drops, oil spills, gemstones, jellyfish, bone, and skeletons."

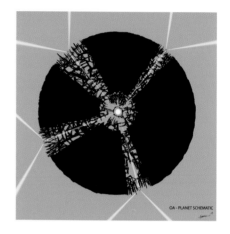

For one of the prominent structures that Hal flies through on his approach to the Central Battery, Moen photographed the inside of a large mushroom cap, then blended it with a mathematically produced mesh to give it an interior architectural skeleton. Various translucent textures were then layered over that and painted. The silhouettes of aliens walking within give it a sense of scale.

Moen's paintings became valuable assets for the visual effects team, which would recreate her landscapes in 3-D space using some of the geometric structures provided by the art department. They would then apply her foreground, mid-ground, and background textures of land formations, structures, skies, clouds, and mist, directly onto their 3-D digital environment. "It was a relatively new idea to generate almost complete matte paintings in the art department prior to post-production, but it helped maintain the vision of the production designer, who is usually no longer on the film once the cameras stop rolling."

The most significant landmark and focal point of Oa is the majestic Central Battery. In the comics, the colossal lantern that harnesses the Green Energy rests on the surface of the planet. This was also the case for the film, albeit for a short while. Although the design went through several iterations, production designer Grant Major always maintained that the Central Battery should be both functional and cinematic in scope. Consequently, he patterned it after a lighthouse, and likened the Battery's Green Energy, which emanates up into space, to a lighthouse's bright beacon, which cuts through the dark, dense fog of hopelessness and fear. That ability to concentrate light from a continuous source and then focus it into multiple directions appealed to Major, as did the multi-faceted, bottled design of its traditional Fresnel lens.

The idea to relocate the Central Battery from the surface to the very center of the planet emerged at a design meeting with another round of illustrations. One in particular, by James Lima, was a study of the Great

Above top: *Planet Oa concept illustration by Michele Moen.*

Above middle: *Planet Oa schematic by Henrick Tamm.*

Above bottom: *This early concept illustration of the Great Hall by James Lima first proposed the idea of a cavernous planet core with the Central Battery located in its center.*

Top: *The Central Battery, deep within the planet's core. Concept illustration by Michele Moen.*

Above: *Early concept illustration depicts the Central Battery on the surface of Oa. Artist: Rodolfo Damagio.*

Above: *Final Oan concept illustration by Michele Moen features the entrance to the Central Battery, dubbed 'Sacre Coeur' by the filmmakers. The Guardian Citadel can be seen in the distance, left of frame. The multiple ships appearing throughout Oa were designed by Paul Ozzimo.*

GREEN LANTERN
MMOEN   082010

Far left: *The visual effects team assembled this early look of Oa for the film's first theatrical trailer. Note that Hal and Tomar are overlooking the 'Sacre Coeur' from a veranda. In the film, it is masterfully revealed at the culmination of an epic fly-through around the Oan city.*

Near left: *Multiple individual "layers" come together to make up one painting. Art courtesy Michele Moen.*

Above: *Many artists contributed various elements and ideas that ultimately made up these final concept illustrations of the Great Hall. Art by Fabian Lacey, with James Lima, Henrick Tamm, Alex Laurant, and Christopher Ross.*

Top: *Concept illustration of the Central Battery by Fabian Lacey with Christopher Ross.*

Above: *(left to right) Dion Beebe, Ozzy Inguanzo, and Grant Major on the Ferris Aircraft party set. Photo by François Duhamel.*

Hall where the Green Lantern Corps assemble. In typical Lima fashion, the painting didn't follow any prior concept or convention. In fact, it took Campbell a moment to figure out which side was right side up. "I had this idea that the Central Battery was at the very center of the planet, and that the Green Energy had caused this erosion that had turned the entire planet into a fibrous labyrinth, creating this crazy abstract architecture. Because the Green Lanterns can fly, the horizontal plane was relative to their point of view," explains Lima. Although this was a divergence from the comic, the idea supported the narrative, and Major was confident this was the way to go. "It made sense for it to be at the center of the planet. It would now be able to throw these shafts of light out in six different directions, toward all space sectors. To me, the Central Battery is like the heart, the heart of willpower. It draws in willpower from the universe and pumps it out via these big streams of energy." Campbell was also convinced.

"Starting off with something eccentric like that again, then backward engineering it to make it work, gave it its own logic and purpose," says Major. The idea of erosion also spawned a second look at the Green Energy. "I started to see this energy as being tangible, like water. Water has the ability to erode rock, and in this case I can see that over countless millennia this willpower has etched out its own space inside this chamber in the middle of the planet," explains Major.

Consequently, the focal point of the city, which was initially planned to be the Central Battery, became the entrance leading down to it. "We call the structure 'Sacre Coeur,'" says Moen. "It was influenced by how Paris was built up around the base of that historic monument. Since the entrance to the Central Battery would have been one of the first structures built, we wanted it to convey a classical sense of nobility and history. The architecture of the dome holding the colossal Fresnel-type lenses was based on the United States Capitol building and London's Royal Albert Hall."

The challenge for Major then became how to reduce the amount of green colored spill light emanating from the giant beams of energy. "For the

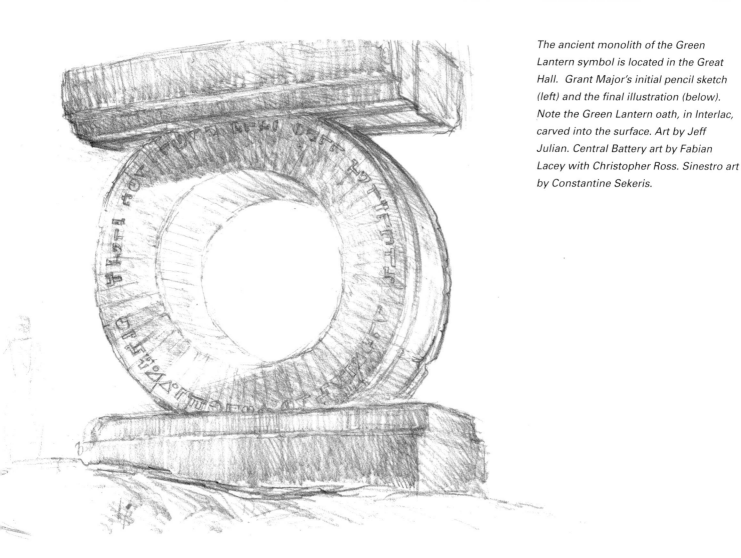

The ancient monolith of the Green Lantern symbol is located in the Great Hall. Grant Major's initial pencil sketch (left) and the final illustration (below). Note the Green Lantern oath, in Interlac, carved into the surface. Art by Jeff Julian. Central Battery art by Fabian Lacey with Christopher Ross. Sinestro art by Constantine Sekeris.

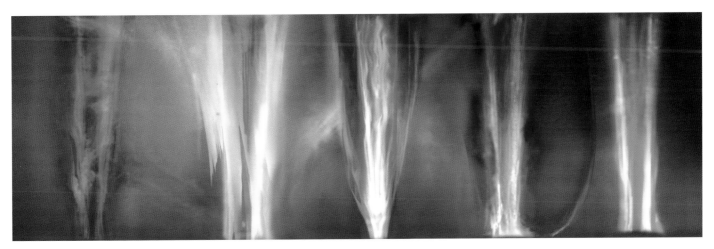

Top: *Tomar leads the first human recruit down into the planet's core. Concept illustration by Fabian Lacey.*

Above: *Studies for the Green Energy beam that emanates out from the "Sacre Coeur." The version in the middle was selected. Concept illustration by Justin Sweet.*

color green to be effective throughout the film, it should be used sparingly," expressed visual effects supervisor Kent Houston at an early development meeting. Director Martin Campbell concurred, and Major worked closely with cinematographer Dion Beebe to achieve the perfect balance. "Dion didn't want everything saturated in green either. Besides, the color gives skin a lifeless complexion when photographed," explains Major. So they devised a way to help reduce the amount of emerald fallout, particularly when the Green Energy discharges from the Power Ring and the Central Battery. "We started playing around with the idea that if the energy had a hotter core, then it would be whiter at the center, and white light is much more radiant than green light," says Major. To also help offset the green, the Oan color palette was kept in the cyan and purple range. As Moen recalls, "Whenever Green Energy was present, its color had to be a particular shade of green, more cyan than yellow." The sickly shade of yellow that represents Parallax and fear was not welcome on Oa.

Sinestro continues speech, mentions inferior human amongst their ranks.

Tomar-Re looks at Hal.

Sinestro...

ANGLE SInestro...

Green Lanterns react to Sinestro's speech. CAMERA TILTS DOWN TO REVEAL...

...Kilowog.

CAMERA MOVES TIGHT on Sinestro.

...as he finishes his speech.

...looking down on the alien Green Lanterns as they...

...raise their rings up towards the camera.

...On another group of Green Lanterns...

...as more rings are thrust into the air.

High up and behind Sinestro, looking out at the congregation...

...the light from the rings rises up in a wave. CAMERA TILTS UP...

as the light continues to rise... CAMERA CONTINUES TILTING UP.

CAMERA CONTINUES TILT UP as the light rises from Oa's core.

High above the city...

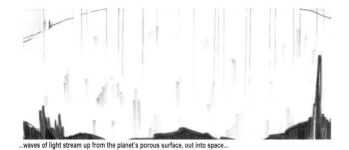

...waves of light stream up from the planet's porous surface, out into space...

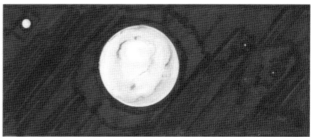

Oa's green light swells...

...and spreads throughout the universe.

Left and top: *Storyboard excerpts, GREAT HALL sequence (Scene 70 / Shots 100-200 / October 23, 2009). Storyboard Artist: Eric Ramsey.*

Above: *Early concept illustration of Planet Oa by Michele Moen.*

THE GREEN LANTERN CORPS

Deep within the planet's core, the brilliant light from the Central Battery radiates into the cavernous canyon of the Great Hall. Its multilevel platforms of slate are crowded with an exotic array of the most imaginative and legendary characters from the DC comic book series. Bringing to life thousands of Green Lanterns from every space sector of the universe took more than two years and the combined talents and efforts of multiple creature designers, prosthetic makeup effects artists, and visual effects wizards.

An extensive amount of visual development was also required on four of the most endearing characters from the comics; the bird-beaked fish-man, Tomar-Re, the hulking pug-faced rhino, Kilowog, the formidable crimson-skinned Thaal Sinestro, and Hal Jordan's magenta-hued predecessor Abin Sur.

One of the first illustrated portraits of Tomar-Re, by illustrator Constantine Sekeris, became one of the most enduring character designs of the film. "As soon as we saw that beautiful, thoughtful face, we all fell in love with it," exclaims costume designer Ngila Dickson, who used photographic reference of South American caiman lizards as inspiration for Tomar's pearlescent, jewel-like skin, which blushes red to indicate his anger. This wink at fans, touches upon the role that color plays within the bigger Green Lantern comic book mythology.

To further help bring this iconic character to life; creature designer Neville Page came aboard, (*Avatar, Star Trek*, and *Cloverfield*). Page modeled the character in ZBrush, while Sekeris and illustrator Simon Thorpe worked with Dickson to design a costume for the tall, slender character who exudes elegance and beauty, and serves as stark contrast to his grisly colleague Kilowog.

Hal Jordan's 8-foot-tall no-nonsense drill sergeant began to take shape under creature designer Aaron Sims (*Sucker Punch, Clash of the Titans*), who established the tone and realism of the character with his team of artists. "He has a very pug dog kind of face, which at a certain point can look very cartoony if you're not careful, so the fleshy jowls around the mouth were the most tricky," explains Sims, who also added the armor-plated rhino-like pelt to the character's bulky anatomy. Taking over from

Above left: *Ngila Dickson's initial costume design for Tomar by illustrator Simon Thorpe.*

Above right: *Evolution of Tomar-Re: 1.) 3-D textured model by Neville Page. 2.) Ngila Dickson's costume design was grafted onto Page's model by Constantine Sekeris 2a.) Suggesting the character's propensity to blush, indicating his mood.*

Right: *This eye line chart created by Andrew Jones establishes the varying height differences the filmmakers had to keep in mind while shooting scenes with the digitally generated Green Lanterns, Kilowog and Tomar-Re. Actor Ryan Reynolds performed the scenes on set with Kilowog stand-in Spencer Wilding and Tomar-Re stand-in Dorian Kingi. The fully digital characters would later be realized in post-production by Jim Berney's visual effects team at Sony Pictures Imageworks.*

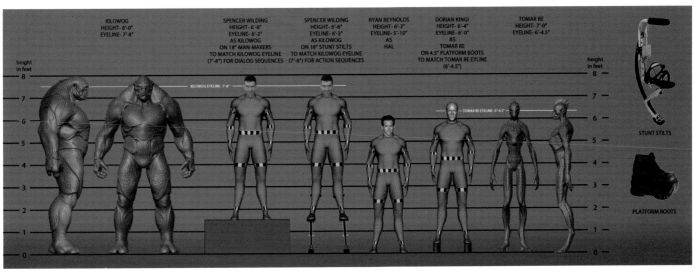

Sims, Page then developed Kilowog's initial body movement and facial expressions, adding lips, skin pigmentation, eye color, and other nuances to the character, like beard stubble. "This is a tough guy, but you don't want him to appear thuggish, so when you add features like a five o'clock shadow it humanizes him," explains Page.

Production designer Grant Major credits Dickson for leading the charge on many of these characters, especially Abin Sur and Sinestro. Dickson refers to her design for Abin as "an elegant river of lines." While she managed to stay faithful to the source material, she added a minor visual cue. "I wanted Abin's Green Lantern suit to convey a regal, almost princely quality. He's the first Green Lantern we see in the film, and I wanted him to be a noble contrast to Hal Jordan. It needed to convey the impression that he wasn't easily replaceable," she says.

The most infamous of all Green Lanterns is the one who becomes the most sinister and evolves into one of greatest villains in the DC Universe. When Dickson set out to design Sinestro's Green Lantern suit, the first thing she did was revisit Hal Jordan's suit. "I always wanted them to mirror each other in appearance, yet keep them generationally apart. Sinestro's suit reflects an older, authoritarian design with very militaristic lines. I always referred to him as the alien Prussian," Dickson quips. She also collaborated closely with Major, Academy Award-winning prosthetics makeup effects department head Joel Harlow, and Mark Strong to craft the overall look for Sinestro. The development process involved multiple makeup and wig camera tests, and mustache variations. "We were all quite bemused by the idea of Sinestro turning into a mustachioed villain. It could be quite hammy if you're not careful, and we tried many different mustaches, but in the end we came back to the original. Now I can't imagine it any other way," she says. A battle scar was added down the contour of Sinestro's face as an indication of his combat experience.

For prosthetics makeup effects supervisor Richie Alonzo, who applied the Sinestro makeup onto Mark Strong, the process took just over three hours. "His look is so refined and so clean that you needed to take the time. Not too many people realize that he wore several prosthetic appliances: A top-of-the-head piece that raised his head a little over an inch and that brought out the front portion to help nail that distinct Sinestro profile, a forehead appliance, and ear tips." Once the tinted silicon pieces were applied, multiple layers of coloration were then added, continues Alonzo. "There were about six other colors in the magenta-fuchsia range that were then airbrushed and spattered on to create the illusion of skin pigmentation. After the hairpieces were on, we airbrushed a shadow tone around the wig to give him a shaved look."

A casting call by director Martin Campbell seeking the most popular and visceral Green Lanterns from the comic book series kicked off the design process for the Green Lantern Corps. The long list was carefully narrowed down to the twenty-five featured extras that would be adapted for the film. The mid-ground and background Green Lanterns seen mostly in wide shots are merely computer reconfigurations of the principal twenty-five. Fleshing out these otherworldly characters would be Neville Page, who with co-designer Tully Summers rendered out a minimum of four to six fully sculpted sketches of each character per day. "My creature career has been based on doing really sound, plausible biology, so this was really out of my comfort zone, but that's the part I liked the most. The challenge here was to give them the appearance of feeling biologically sound, even if there were huge leaps of faith about the various physiognomy of these characters," says Page.

Top left: *Initial concept illustration of Kilowog by The Aaron Sims Company.*

Bottom left: *Image of Neville Page's 3-D model of Kilowog.*

Right: *Final Kilowog design by Neville Page. Ngila Dickson's costume design illustrated by Constantine Sekeris.*

KILOWOG
SKIN TREATMENT 3
HAIR
EYE SHAPE 3
EYE COLOR 4

IMAGE # 9

Left: *A closer look at Kilowog's facial features by Neville Page reveals beard stubble. "When you add features like a five o'clock shadow it humanizes him," explains Page.*

Right: *Final concept art of Thaal Sinestro illustrated by Constantine Sekeris. For Sinestro, Ngila Dickson revisited her design for Hal Jordan's suit. "I always wanted them to mirror each other in appearance, yet keep them generationally apart. SInestro's suit reflects an older, authoritarian design with very militaristic lines."*

Top left: *Martin Campbell preps actor Mark Strong prior to filming. Photo by François Duhamel.*

Middle left: *Sinestro mustache options. Art by Constantine Sekeris.*

Bottom left: *Early hairpiece designs for Sinestro ran the gamut. A militaristic buzz cut was chosen. Art by Constantine Sekeris.*

SINESTRO MUSTACHE OPTIONS

01 02 03 04

Above: *Prosthetics makeup effects supervisor Richie Alonzo applies the Sinestro makeup onto Mark Strong. The process took just over three hours. "His look is so refined and so clean that you needed to take the time. Not too many people realize that he wore several prosthetic appliances" Photo courtesy Joel Harlow.*

01A 02A 03A 04A

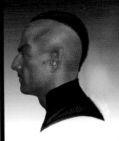

01B

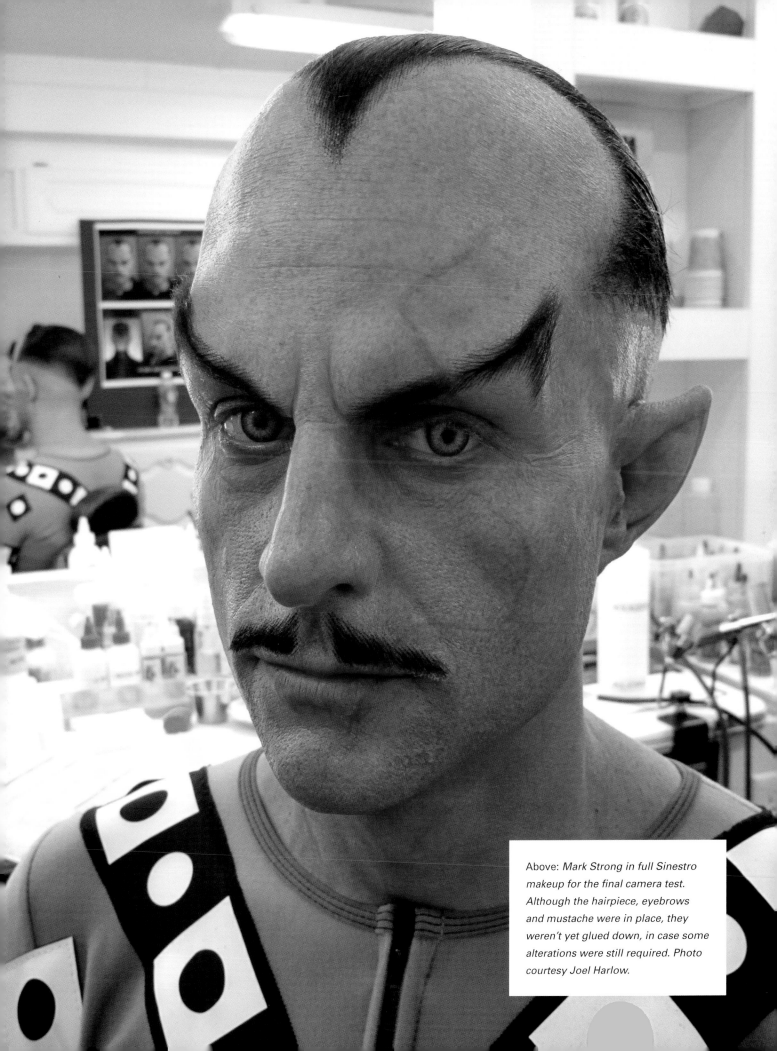

Above: Mark Strong in full Sinestro makeup for the final camera test. Although the hairpiece, eyebrows and mustache were in place, they weren't yet glued down, in case some alterations were still required. Photo courtesy Joel Harlow.

Opposite: *The Green Lantern G'hu was a former prison guard who single-handedly quelled a riot. He is armored with a crustacean-like shell, and everything about him is built to cut, rip, and hurt. Early 3-D sketch (top left) and final design (bottom left) by Neville Page and Tully Summers.*

Opposite, top right: *Early 3-D sketch of Salaak by Neville Page and Tully Summers.*

Opposite, bottom right: *Final design for the cyclopean slug Larvox by Neville Page and Tully Summers.*

Top: *Sinestro comes to life in this scene from the film.*

Above: *Cinematographer Dion Bebee dollies into a shot with Ryan Reynolds, Dorian Kingi, and Mark Strong. Note the cardboard cutouts standing in for the Guardians. Photo by François Duhamel.*

Constructing Green Lantern: From Page to Screen

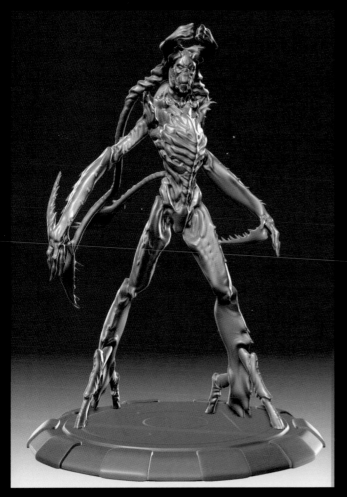

TULLY SUMMERS   G'HU V1   10·9·9   TULLY SUMMERS   SALAAK V1   10·9·9

KILOWOG ON OA/ GREEN LANTERN / JUSTIN SWEET 09

Each character was meticulously researched, with biographies and comic book artwork provided to Page and Summers to inform their work. "The bios were very interesting to me because it gave us some forethought as to who these characters are supposed to be," notes Page, who likens his approach to that of an actor. "If you're an actor with a small part and not a whole lot of lines, your responsibility is to look for details in the script and create a back-story for your character. As a character designer your obligation is very similar. You are creating a character like an actor would, and you look for opportunities that will give you either a performance cue or an aesthetic cue. If we know that the Oan crypt keeper Morro eats lunch alone, we can imply he's anti-social."

The cyclopean slug Larvox was one of Page's favorites. "I'm assuming when they called him Larvox, they were referring to larva, and there were indications in the comics that it was larval in feel, so that became visual reference for him." Another Green Lantern, Norchavius, the protector of Space Sector 26, is written as a renowned sculptor, so Page infused that aesthetic cue into the character by giving his body a sculptural form. "His head and certain body parts are automotive-inspired. It's got all the same form language a car would have." In contrast, Green Lantern Rot Lop Fan's awkward hammer-shaped body seemed to have no rationale. "Nothing explained his hunch, the squareness of his head, or the two masses on his shoulders. We initially thought they were oxygen tanks, but the fact that he's blind and communicates acoustically allowed us to see them as huge tympanic membranes, like what a frog would have as ears. We made them into these large gelatinous filled tympanic sacks that create and receive sound." For other iconic Green Lanterns like Apros, Page says, smiling, "You just gotta make it feel more alien and less floating pumpkin."

Designing the ladies of the Corps allowed for a brief respite from the slippery, slimy, scaly beasts. The delicate balance between preserving the femme fatale physique while instilling them with an otherworldly

Above: *Kilowog instructs a group of Green Lantern trainees in this early concept illustration by Justin Sweet.*

Opposite, top left and right: *The winged R'amey Holl by Neville Page and Tully Summers was a respectable interpretation of the character.*

Right: *Early concepts for Kilowog and Boodikka by Justin Sweet.*

appearance sometimes required the artists to take some liberties from the source material. The winged R'amey Holl, for instance, was a respectable reinterpretation of the character. "The obvious would have been to just add butterfly wings to a pin-up girl, but that would have been disappointing," explains Page. One female Lantern that was especially significant to costume designer Ngila Dickson was a young Green Lantern trainee that appeared in an early draft of the script. She was not from the comics and had no name, but Dickson felt that the character represented a strong role model for girls, and envisioned her as a violet-skinned athlete with frizzy sensors for ears. Although the character was cut from the script, Dickson's initial design endured and an original Green Lantern was added to the list of twenty-five featured extras. Her name: N'Gila Grnt. "When I heard *that*, I knew everyone understood how obsessed I had become with that character," jokes Dickson.

Designing individual costumes for each member of the Green Lantern Corps was a unique experience for Dickson, who would receive the bodies from Page in the alien raw. "An important part of making a body look good is how you break it up with a costume," explains Page. The designs of some of those characters made applying the suit concept unbelievably difficult, recalls Dickson. "They were incredibly complex in shape and skin tone, and I'd be sitting there looking at a few of them thinking, how the hell am I going to get a green lantern symbol onto this body. But that's one of the great things about working on a film like this, suddenly you find the ways and means of making all that work, while respecting the design of the creature itself and taking advantage of the things that are really beautiful in them." Page praises the creative spirit and imagination of the original comic book artists. "They really deserve the credit for these creatures. They gave us the core ideas, and even on occasions where we departed from the iconography that was set in the comics, we still tried to retain the original vibe and flare for fans."

Above: *Final design for Boodikka by Neville Page and Tully Summers. Ngila Dickson's costume design illustrated by Constantine Sekeris.*

Left: *Final design for Rot Lop Fan by Neville Page and Tully Summers. The blind Green Lantern communicates acoustically, so the hunches on his back were designed as huge tympanic membranes. "We made them into these large gelatinous sacks that create and resolve sound," explains Page.*

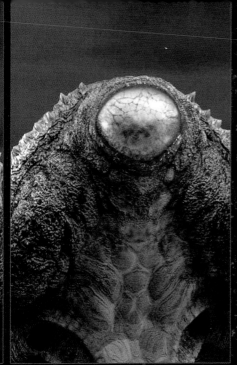

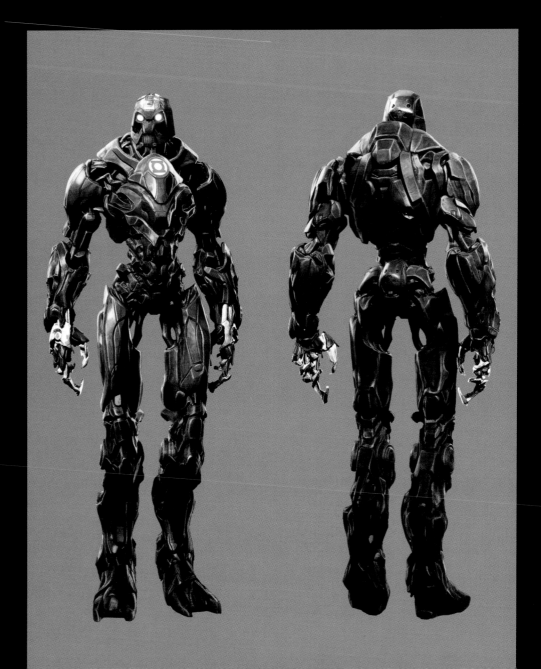

Above: *Cyclopean M'Dahna's nictating membrane. Concept art by Neville Page and Tully Summers.*

Left: *Stel by The Aaron Sims Company. Ngila Dickson's costume design illustrated by Simon Thorpe.*

Opposite: *Final design for the multi-limbed bookkeeper of the Green Lantern Corps, Salaak, by Neville Page and Tully Summers.*

Left: *Final Medphyll design by Neville Page and Tully Summers.*

Below: *Final Norchavius design by Neville Page and Tully Summers was automotive-inspired.*

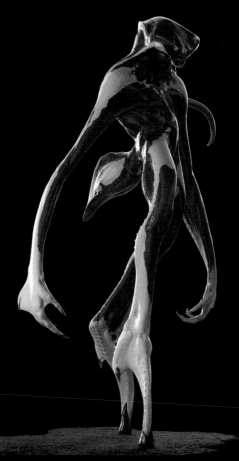

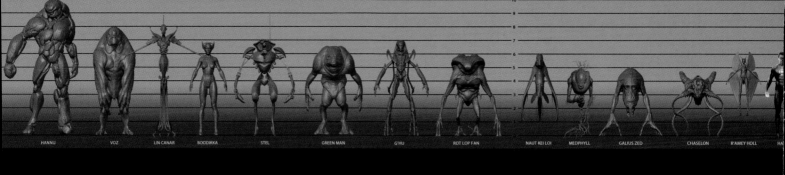

HANNU   VOZ   LIN CANAR   BOODIKKA   STEL   GREEN MAN   G'HU   ROT LOP FAN   NAUT KEI LOI   MEDPHYLL   GALIUS ZED   CHASELON   R'AMEY HOLL   HA

Lin Canar

Princess Iolande

M'Dahna

Naut Kei Loi

Boodikka

G'Hu

Green Man

Salaak

Penelops

N'Gila Grnt

Bzzd

Larvox

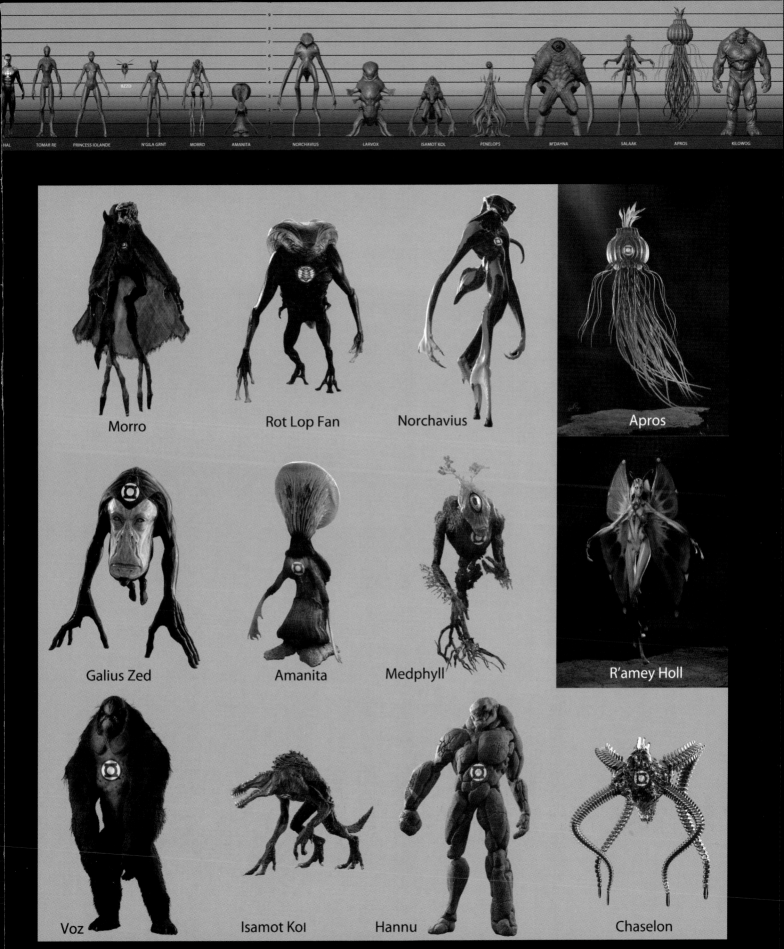

Above: *Green Lantern Corps background extras. Creatures by Neville Page and Tully Summers. Ngila Dickson's costume designs illustrated by Simon Thorpe. Boodikka and Princess Iolande costumes illustrated by Constantine Sekeris.*

THE GUARDIANS AND THE CITADEL

Creature designer Aaron Sims and his team designed ten individual Guardians for the film. The popular characters—Ganthet, Sayd, Scar, and Appa—were directly adapted from the comics, while the other five likenesses were original to the film and selected by director Martin Campbell and producer Donald De Line. Although the designs retain the characters' familiar weathered blue skin and enlarged craniums from the comics— initially modeled after first Israeli Prime Minister David Ben-Gurion—Sims added a translucent membrane around the tops of their heads at production designer Grant Major's behest. "I wanted to give them an astral sense. So the stars are reflected on their heads, but they're also partly within them. In a way, the Guardians are the stars, they are the universe," explains Major.

The Guardian citadel, where the elusive beings remain perpetually cloistered in council, was reimagined for the film as a slightly ominous, imposing tower overlooking the Oan capital. Campbell requested Major make the shape circular, like the ring. "A picture entered my mind of this crown-like shape, with these separate thrones facing each other," recalls Major, who worked closely with concept artist Justin Sweet to realize his vision. "He really made it happen by making it more sculptural and bringing in the obsidian texture," says Major. Sweet's concepts for the individual Guardian thrones imply that they cater to their thought patterns. Sweet explains, "The top shapes of the thrones feel as if they almost wrap around their heads, and the obsidian-type mineral is worn down, as if over the millennia the power of their thoughts have affected it." "Justin also added the lens motif to the surface of the rostrum floor," adds Major. "[Cinematographer] Dion Bebee liked the idea that there was a subtle light source within the architecture, coming up from the center of the planet."

Although the Guardians are roughly four feet tall, they're never seen in relationship to anyone else in the film. "Putting them up on these tall thrones with these long flowing crimson robes gave them more of a graphic presence. In a way, they are the high priests of the universe," explains Major. Achieving the final look for those long flowing robes didn't come easy to costume designer Ngila Dickson, who hit a creative impasse. She turned to assistant costume designers Libby Dempster and Carlos

Rosario for inspiration. "Brilliantly, the next morning all these fabulous ideas were sitting on my desk. I looked and talked through everything with them, and then I just completely put them aside," recalls Dickson. Rosario was deflated at first, but their efforts proved fruitful. "They gave me back my creative energy, *and* they had also brought the lantern. When I saw that, I knew immediately what had to be done," says Dickson, who took concept designer Fabian Lacey's illustration of the Power Battery and immediately began drawing on it. "It's one of the oldest elements on Oa. I took the metal design from the handle and turned it into these terribly restrictive collars. I imagined that when they first put on these robes, they were probably very beautiful creatures, and now they're old and wizened. It gives a sense of weight and mana to the robes, almost holding the Guardians together," explains Dickson.

Sims's 3-D models of the Guardians, along with Dickson's costume designs, and illustrator Michele Moen's matte paintings of the Citadel environment were produced entirely digitally and then released directly to the visual effects team, As for the Citadel itself, Major added a step. He wanted it realized in the physical world first. In fact, the Great Hall also underwent the same process of digital conversion.

"We built a lot of scenic miniatures on *The Lord of the Rings* and *King Kong*, which we then had digitally scanned. I felt that for these two set pieces, I would not be able to achieve the look I wanted without first building them physically," says Major. Visual effects art director Andrew Jones, whose experience included director James Cameron's *Avatar* and Tim Burton's *Alice In Wonderland*, also recognized the technical limitations of producing these particular sets digitally from scratch. "Often times, especially on something sculptural like this, it's extremely difficult to get that amount of detail digitally. Most times they'll just apply a Photoshop texture file over the digital model, and on something this massive a scale, it just never really looks as good as a real physical model," says Jones.

Major and Jones oversaw the process, which began with Sweet's approved concept paintings of the Citadel. Assistant art director Robert Fechtman used them to produce a workable design in the form of technical

Top: *Early throne concept by Justin Sweet.*

Above: *Ngila Dickson's design for the Guardian's crimson robes by Simon Thorpe. Guardian Sayd by The Aaron Sims Company.*

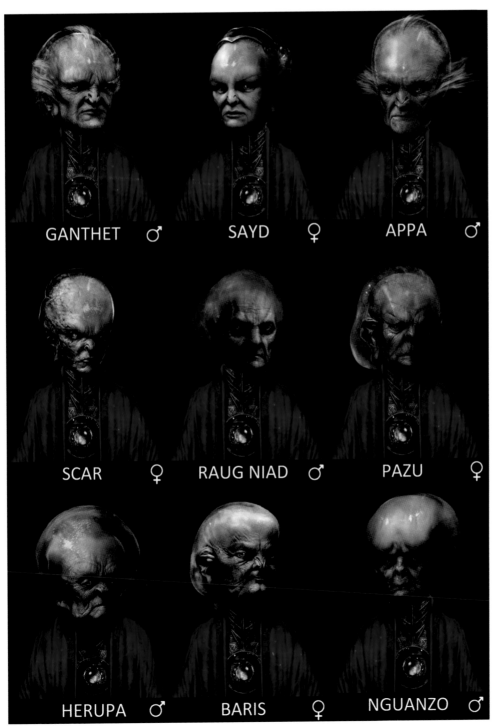

GANTHET ♂   SAYD ♀   APPA ♂

SCAR ♀   RAUG NIAD ♂   PAZU ♀

HERUPA ♂   BARIS ♀   NGUANZO ♂

Top left: *Early Guardian concept by Fabian Lacey. The original comic book Guardians were modeled after the first Prime Minister of Israel, David Ben-Gurion.*

Top right: *Female and male guardian hands by Neville Page, revisions by Jeff Julian.*

Left: *The Guardian Council. Comic book fans will recognize Ganthet, Sayd, Appa, and Scar. Also named in the comics throughout the years: Herupa, Baris, and Pazu. New to the film are Raug Niad, an anagram of the word Guardian, and Nguanzo, discernable to those acquainted with the film's researcher and this book's author. Creatures designed by The Aaron Sims Company. Ngila Dickson's costume designs illustrated by Simon Thorpe.*

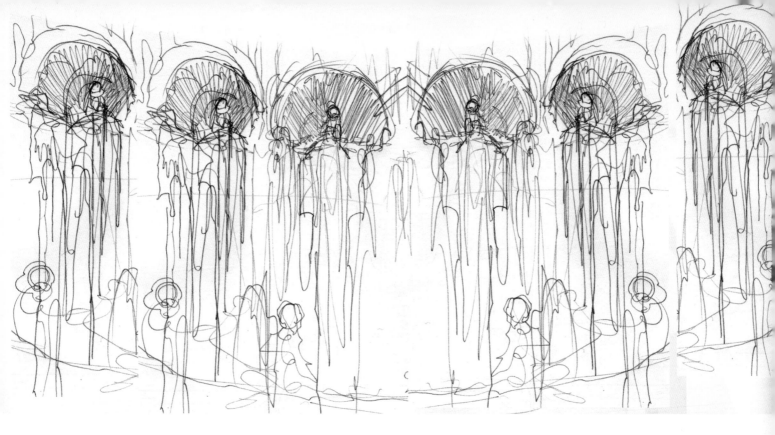

Top: *Rough sketch of the Citadel by Justin Sweet.*

Above: *Sinestro addresses the Guardian council. Concept illustration by Justin Sweet.*

Above: *The Guardians perched high above Oa. Concept illustration by Justin Sweet.*

Right: *Justin Sweet's initial concept for the individual Guardian thrones suggested they cater to their thought patterns. "The obsidian-type mineral is worn down, as if over the millennia the power of their thoughts have affected it," explains Sweet.*

CITADEL VERSION 2 / GREEN LANTERN / JUSTIN 09 / JULIAN 10

Top: *Production designer Grant Major wanted the Citadel to be located high above Oa, almost up in the stars. Final concept illustration by Michele Moen. Citadel art by Justin Sweet, revisions by Jeff Julian.*

Above: *Final concept illustration of the Guardian Citadel by Justin Sweet, revisions by Jeff Julian. The subtle green light illuminating the architecture and rostrum floor from within emanates up from the Central Battery.*

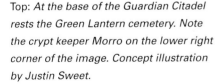

Top: *At the base of the Guardian Citadel rests the Green Lantern cemetery. Note the crypt keeper Morro on the lower right corner of the image. Concept illustration by Justin Sweet.*

Above left: *Morro's staff was adapted directly from the comics by Jeff Julian. Morro by Neville Page and Tully Summers.*

Above right: *Early cemetery concept art by Justin Sweet.*

drawings, including actual dimensions. The rostrum is forty feet in diameter; the Guardians sit twenty-six feet above that dais, and the Citadel tower rises two thousand feet above the base of the Oan cemetery plateau. In most instances, the art department produced digital 3-D models of the sets internally before turning them over to the pre-visualization department. However, in this case Fechtman's drawings were handed over directly to the "pre-vis" team, headed by Kyle Robinson. Robinson's modelers built a rough digital model of the Citadel in three-dimensional space, with scaled figures of the characters on the set.

Once approved by Major and Campbell, Jones took the approved specifications to sculptors Jamie Miller and Steve Pinney. Miller and four assistants built the massive model of the Great Hall at 3/4-inch scale, casting real rocks and minerals, then used the skins from those molds. Some actual rocks even made it into the miniature. "At that scale, you got a lot of detail very quickly from these rocks," explains Jones.

For the Guardian Citadel, Pinney needed to realize two miniatures, the entire tower at 1/4-inch scale, and a more detailed tower top and thrones at 3/4-inch scale. Jones brought Pinney four small sample shards of black obsidian, concerned that there was no material they could cast that could

This spread: *Final concept illustration of the Guardian Citadel and Green Lantern cemetery by Justin Sweet.*

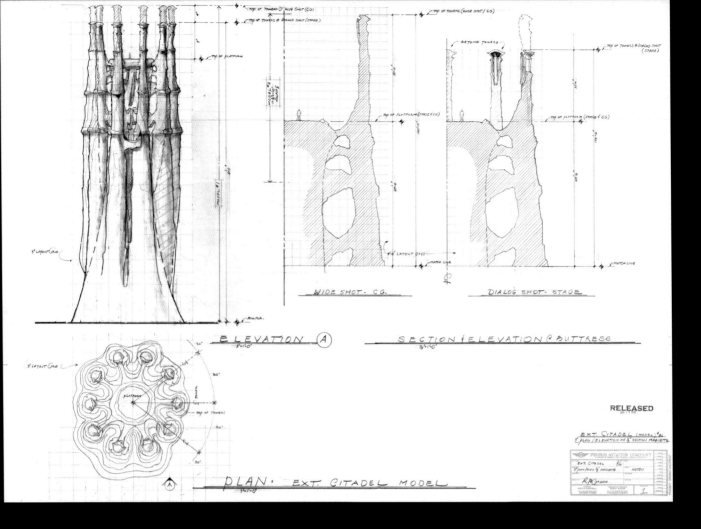

Top: *Plan and elevations of the Guardian Citadel. Drawing by Robert Fechtman.*

Above: *Early concept of the Guardian citadel and 'Sacre Coeur' in the distance. Artist: Justin Sweet.*

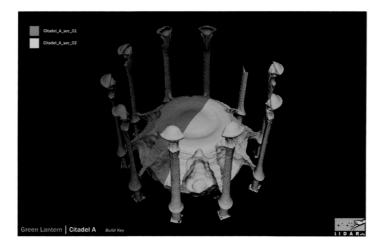

Top left: *Competed 1/4-inch scale miniature of the Guardian citadel by Steve Pinney. Photo by Ozzy Inguanzo.*

Top right: *High-resolution 3-D lidar scan of the 3/4-inch Citadel miniature.*

Bottom right: *Sculptor Steve Pinney attaches the Guardians to their thrones, completing his work on the 3/4-inch miniature. Photo by Ozzy Inguanzo.*

replicate the obsidian in those huge amounts that they needed in order to build the model. The following week, when Jones returned to the shop, there was one extra obsidian piece on the table. "Steve said, 'I think one of them broke in half, because you only gave me four pieces,'" recalls Jones, who looked at each of them, baffled. "Then Steve said, 'Is it that third one?' I picked it up, but it was the same one I had brought him. Steve said, 'Squeeze it.' I stuck my nail in it and it was clay. I was completely fooled," Jones recalls, laughing. Pinney had come up with a process to replicate the obsidian texture out of clay, and sculpted both Citadel miniatures by hand. "He used a ring tool, which he'd scrape through the clay to make a concave gauge, but as he went through he'd rattle it to make those imperfections that you get in obsidian. It was very effective," recalls Jones. Visual effects spent a week scanning the miniatures in detail using a high-resolution, three-dimensional Lidar scan that converted them into digital models. "There's just no other way we could have achieved this look," says Jones proudly.

CITADEL BATTLE/ GREEN LANTERN / JUSTIN SWEET 2009

CONSTRUCTING WILL

Left: *Green Lantern's energy. Concept illustration by Seth Engstrom.*

Below: *Research & Development: Lead set designer William Hunter poses with the projected laser beams. Photos by Seth Engstrom.*

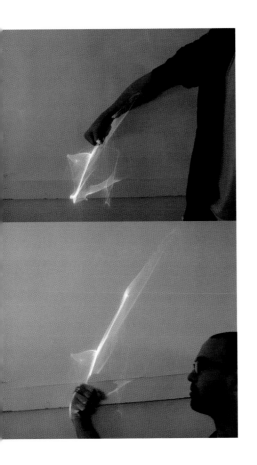

Fueled by willpower, a Green Lantern's Power Ring grants its selected bearer the ability to wield the extraordinary power of the Green Energy. Mentally triggered, the Power Ring can generate a Green Lantern's suit and flight capabilities, plus a vast array of battle tools, from concussive ring-blasts to solid-light constructs, anything the wearer's imagination can conjure up and willpower can sustain.

While there have been a variety of energy effects visualized in past films and other media, the Green Energy needed to be unique, powerful, and threatening; an iconic signature for the character. Production designer Grant Major wanted the Green Energy to feel tangible and real. "There needed to be logic and physics involved, otherwise it just became too magical," explains Major.

To design this roiling energy and its multiple manifestations, he turned to concept artist Seth Engstrom, who, along with visual effects art director Andrew Jones, developed the look of the energized willpower for the film. In fact, they wrote the book on it; a twenty-one page style guide for the visual effects team. "When Seth came along he really changed the landscape of it and took on what I was hoping to get. Something that was more than just projected light," recalls Major. "In the comics, the Green Energy is usually over the top and the constructs are bold and graphic, which adapts wonderfully to the printed page. We needed to take that familiar concept and bring it into the real world without it looking cheesy or magical, rather giving it a mature science-like credibility that is uniquely cool and deserving for Green Lantern's film debut," says Engstrom.

Some preliminary illustrations had been generated based on the look of plasma, but they were missing a sense of energy and movement. "Plasma looks calm, soft, nice, and we had all seen it before in conventional effects. So we started doing our own experiments with things that we couldn't find through conventional means," says Engstrom. The film's model maker, Brett Phillips, showed up at the art department one day with a fun psychedelic light dome that he had created for parties. He set up a similar display in Engstrom's office by shooting a green laser pen into a crumpled piece of Mylar. "It refracted these amazing streaks of light onto the wall, random patterns that we just couldn't have thought up ourselves," explains Engstrom.

Jones experimented further with the laser, projecting it through and off of different objects, such as obsidian and quartz rock samples, and also firing it at a small moving cylinder wrapped in crumpled Mylar. "Andrew was now producing these animated shapes that were morphing and changing in a three-dimensional way. It seemed to cap-ture what we wanted the Green Energy to look like," says Engstrom. They videotaped and photographed these unique patterns, building a library of "energy" elements that Engstrom would later import into Photoshop to manipulate further. Other added references included certain macro and super slow-motion photography that captured movement: paint splats, liquids, bullets being fired, and explosions, to name a few. He even took photos of toothpaste splatters on his bathroom mirror at home. Slow-motion photography of a pocket lighter being ignited served as reference for the chaotic initial spark of the Green Energy discharging from the Power Ring. Engstrom then expertly synthesized all of these elements in Photoshop, yielding the unique and powerful design language for the Green Energy.

With the overall look approved, Engstrom was now tasked with adapting it to specific conditions called out in the script. These illustrations, referred to as key frames, represent a snapshot of a seminal moment in the film, everything from the charging of the Power Battery to Hal Jordan's constructs, even individual ring-blasts (over 60 variations were produced). Each of these key frames served as a guide for the actors and crew on set, as well as the visual effects artists who would later need to replicate the design digitally.

Additionally, director Martin Campbell requested that each Green Lantern have his or her own energy signature. That meant taking the energy design that had been developed and using it to create specific energy auras, flying trails, constructs and ring-blasts unique to each of the primary Green Lanterns. "Martin wanted Kilowog's energy to resemble heavy chains, so his aura and flying pattern is heavier and thicker in design. Tomar-Re is more intellectual and professorial, so his signature reflects precise and complex geometric patterns. Abin Sur and Sinestro are two of the most advanced Lanterns, and their energy is very clean and precise. Sinestro's construct energy is particularly sharp and lethal, thin like his moustache," says Engstrom.

Hal Jordan's energy vernacular primarily revolves around aircraft, his flying pattern resembling the wingtip vortices trailing off a jet's wings. The director also wanted Jordan's energy to reflect the character's progression as a Lantern, from novice to expert. Engstrom breaks it down: "The look for Hal's energy is based on his skill level, from his early chaotic and uncontrollable patterns of energy, ramping up through the course of the film to a more clean, precise, and perfectly focused look."

Campbell, Major, and Dickson were also keen on integrating the Green Energy into the Green Lantern suit. "We're using the energy in conjunction with the suit to illustrate how it all works. The energy is triggered by Hal's willpower and imagination, so we first see the suit glow faintly from within as the energy is called up. Then it quickly travels down

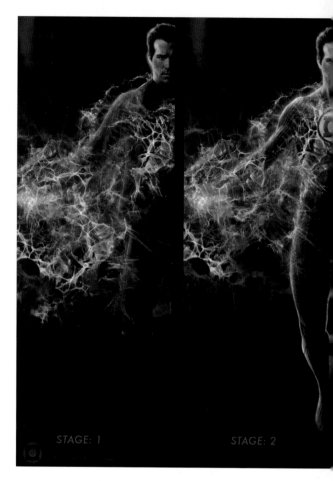

STAGE: 1   STAGE: 2

Above: *Martin Campbell wanted Hal Jordan's energy to reflect the character's skill level as a Green Lantern, from the uncontrollable patterns of a novice to the perfectly focused willpower of an expert. "You have to create a logic to it. There has to be a set of rules, otherwise you have nothing to lock on to," explains Campbell. Concept illustrations by Seth Engstrom.*

Right: *These renderings by Seth Engstrom depict unique energy flight trails for each of the primary Green Lanterns.*

STAGE: 3   STAGE: 4   STAGE: 5

GREEN LANTERN - ENERGY

Sinestro

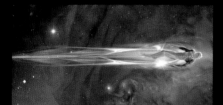

Tomar-Re

Hal Jordan

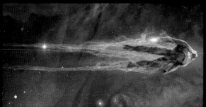

Kilowog

GREEN ENERGY
SLOW FLYING/HOVERING   V002
HAL JORDAN

ENERGY: STREAKS FROM THE FASTER MOVING PARTS OF THE
BODY. THIS IS A VERY SUBTLE GREEN STRAFE, MAINLY FROM THE RING.
THIS ENERGY IS SEEN WHEN STOPPING, TAKING OFF, STRONG
MOVEMENTS WHILE FIGHTING, OR SUDDEN MOVEMENT, AND DISAPPEARS QUICKLY.

BODY GLOW: AS IN THE COMIC, A GLOW AROUND THE BODY IS SEEN WHILE
USING ENERGY. HERE THE GLOW IS VERY VERY SUBTLE, SEEN IN INTERMITTENT
SPOTS, AND NOT EVENLY AROUND THE WHOLE BODY. IT MOSTLY APPEARS ON THE
OPPOSITE SIDE OF THE MOTION.

Top left: *Seth Engstrom's concept illustration and detailed description for Green Lantern's energy trails.*

Bottom left: *Martin Campbell directs Ryan Reynolds during the training sequence shoot. Photo by François Duhamel.*

TOMAR RE

SINESTRO

Top: *Seth Engstrom crafted a unique energy signature for each of the primary Green Lanterns.*

Above: *Kilowog sizes up his new pupil.*

his arm, buried in the tiny grooves and cracks of the suit until it reaches the Power Ring and projects out a ring-blast or construct," explains Major.

"In the comics it's a beam of light that seems to effortlessly come out of the ring and construct an object, almost like something a magician easily could do. We needed to show a certain amount of effort, strength, and willpower required to make a construct," says Major. Andrew Jones collaborated with Engstrom and the pre-visualization team to develop a credible way to realize the constructs for the film. Jones explains, "We hypothesized that the Green Energy is discharged from the wearer, via the Power Ring, into the ether, and once it's out there his thoughts transform it into an object with tangible qualities. Seth's illustrations of the Gatling gun construct demonstrates the process best. Like a reverse explosion, the Gatling gun starts congealing out from the ether in a series of components, and consolidates into something that looks solid, but had a signature Green Energy appearance to it. When it disappears, we didn't want it to go uniformly, but in a way that took into account the object's solidity. The more solid bits that took longer to produce would take longer to dissipate." Jones adds, "The final element in achieving a realistic look to a construct or ring-blast is making sure it interacts strongly with its surrounding environment, with the performer's body, and with the atmosphere, and that's what we were trying to achieve."

This visual complexity and effort required for a Green Lantern to make and sustain a construct conveys a sense of verisimilitude, first established in the training sequence when Jordan is tested and taken through his paces. "Once you take away the magic, you need to obey certain rules, and suddenly it's more believable. Hal gets kicked around and needs to learn how to make constructs quickly, how to make the right construct, and how to focus his willpower to sustain a construct," notes Major. Jordan also learns that there is another force that draws on another type of energy: a fear-based yellow energy that is seemingly immune to the power of green, and the only way to overcome this deadly force is to conquer fear itself.

HAL CLOTHING TRANSFORMATION
STARTING FROM INSIDE THE GL SUIT, THE EXTERIOR FORMS
LIKE A CONSTRUCT AROUND THE SKIN, THEN HARD FORMING
AROUND HIS BODY. (THE NORMAL SUIT IS A TASTEFUL SHADE OF GREEN)

Top left: *Green Lantern suit transformation. Concept illustration by Seth Engstrom.*

Middle left: *Green Lantern emerges over the Ferris Aircraft celebration, marking his first public appearance. Note the wingtip vortices left in his wake. Art by Seth Engstrom.*

Bottom left: *Early concept rendering of a construct training exercise above the Training Platforms on Oa. Art by Rodolfo Damaggio.*

Right: *Ring blast progression. Seth Engstrom's concept illustrations with accompanying descriptions served as guide for the shooting crew on set, and the visual effects team in post-production.*

GREEN ENERGY
RING BLAST - PROGRESSION OF ENERGY
STAGE 1
HAL JORDAN

GREEN ENERGY ACTION:
DURING A RING BLAST, A SLIGHT
TRACE OF ENERGY FROM WITHIN THE LANTERNS BODY IS
SEEN, TO VISUALLY SHOW THAT THE ENERGY CREATED, IS
COMING FROM HIS WILL.

THE PROGRESSION STARTS WITH
GREEN FROM THE EYES, INSIDE THE PUPIL.

THEN FROM UNDER THE SUIT, SEEN WITHIN THE
IMPRESSION LINES, GREEN ENERGY MOVES FROM THE
HEAD.

STAGE 2

IN A FLASH, THE ENERGY WITH THE BODY, MOVES TO
THE THE RING, FOLLOWING THE LINES OF THE SUIT.

STAGE 3

THE ENERGY FLOWS TO THE RING, IGNITING THE RING, AND
SENDING OUT THE BLAST, IN THE BLAST TYPE THAT HAS
BEEN WILLED BY THE LANTERN.

THIS ALL HAPPENS VERY QUICKLY. THE ENERGY SHOWN IS
DEPENDENT ON THE LANTERN'S SUIT.

THERE IS ALSO A SLIGHT PLASMA LIKE FLAIR
SEEN WITH THE LINES, TO SHOW THAT IT
IS GREEN ENERGY, AND NOT JUST LIGHT.

This page: *Early concepts for the Green Lantern Training Platforms on Oa. Illustration by Rodolfo Damaggio (top), and Ed Natividad (middle and bottom).*

This page: *Developing the fist construct:
Early concept by Justin Sweet and Alex
Laurant was well received, but ultimately
too solid and too electrical (top). Seth
Engstrom kept the fist end solid, while
the rest trailed off erratically (middle).
Final fist construct by Sony Pictures
Imageworks, as seen in the film (bottom).*

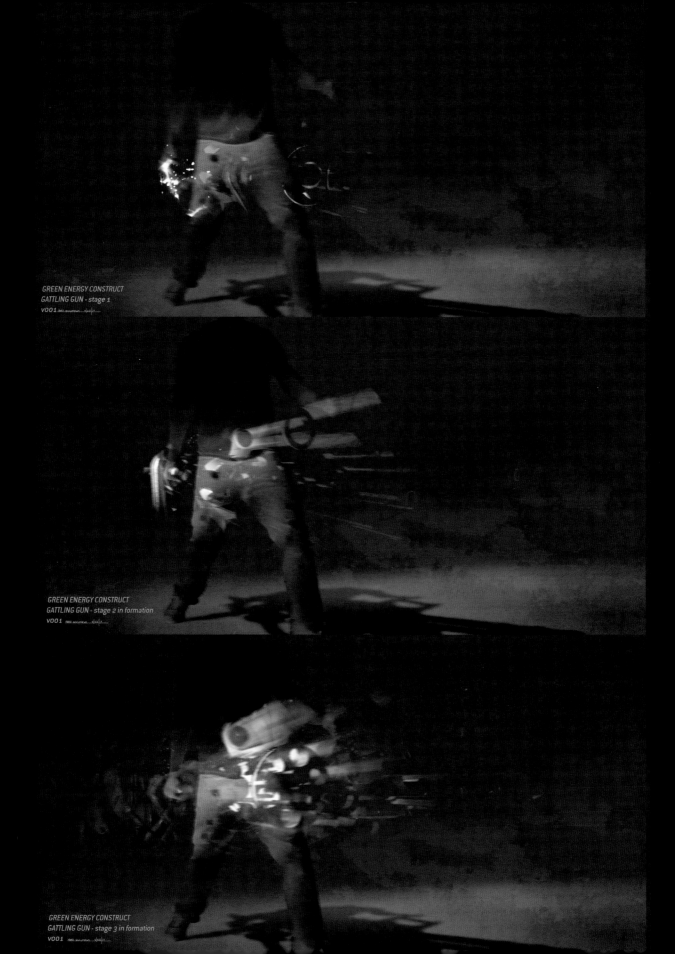

GREEN ENERGY CONSTRUCT
GATTLING GUN - stage 1
VOO1

GREEN ENERGY CONSTRUCT
GATTLING GUN - stage 2 in formation
VOO1

GREEN ENERGY CONSTRUCT
GATTLING GUN - stage 3 in formation
VOO1

GREEN ENERGY CONSTRUCT
GATTLING GUN - stage 4 in formation
VOO1

GREEN ENERGY CONSTRUCT
GATTLING GUN - Stage 5 - FULLY FORMED
VOO1

GREEN ENERGY CONSTRUCT
GATTLING GUN - Stage 6 - Form Disintegrating
VOO1

GREEN ENERGY CONSTRUCT
Hal's First Try - Failed Construct
V002 SETH ENGSTROM 5.6.10

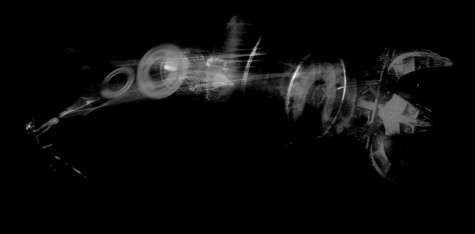

ED NATIVIDAD
10.16.09
GREEN LANTERN
GL FX 011

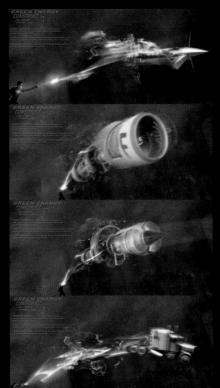

Pages 152–153: *Seth Engstroms's final concept illustrations of a Gatling gun demonstrates the progression of a construct.*

Top: *Early concept for a "failed" construct implied Hal Jordan's lack of concentrated willpower. Illustration by Seth Engstrom.*

Above left: *Early concept by Ed Natividad shows a construct forming bit by bit.*

Above right: *Various constructs taking shape. Concept illustrations by Seth Engstrom.*

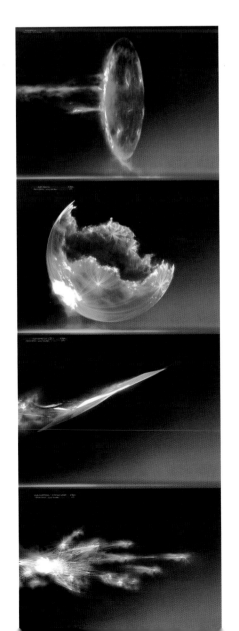

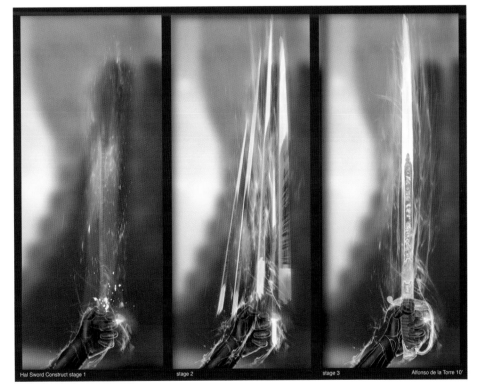

Top: *An out-of-control helicopter hurtling through a crowd is enveloped by shafts of green energy that solidify around it, creating a giant hot rod construct. Illustration by Seth Engstrom.*

Left: *Early construct studies by James Clyne. (Top to bottom) Shield, Air Bag, Sword, Geometric Structure.*

Above: *Hal's sword construct was based on Martin Jordan's saber insignia from his flight jacket. Concept illustration by Alfonso de la Torre.*

A panicking guest in front of her falls --

-- tripping her.

Carol crashes onto the stage --

-- into the drum kit.

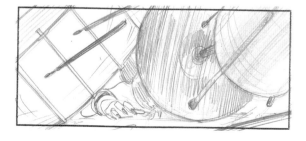

The helicopter thunders towards lens.

Carol reacts in horror.

The helicopter is coming straight at her.

GL's fist up into shot. The ring flashes:

Suddenly, a (green construct) Hot Wheels car evolves foreground.

The stricken helicopter shoots up onto the car, forming a 'copter-car.

-- propelling it forward.

-- saving Carol's life.

The 'copter-car shoots out of frame.

The 'copter-car shoots up a 'construct' of a Hot Wheels track --

This spread: *Storyboard excerpts, FERRIS PARTY sequence (Scenes 89 / Shots 510-610 / June 1, 2010). Storyboard artists: Collin Grant and Eric Ramsey.*

Below: *Director Martin Campbell's* Green Lantern *script—or "the bible," as he refers to it—with his hand-written notes. Photo by Ozzy Inguanzo.*

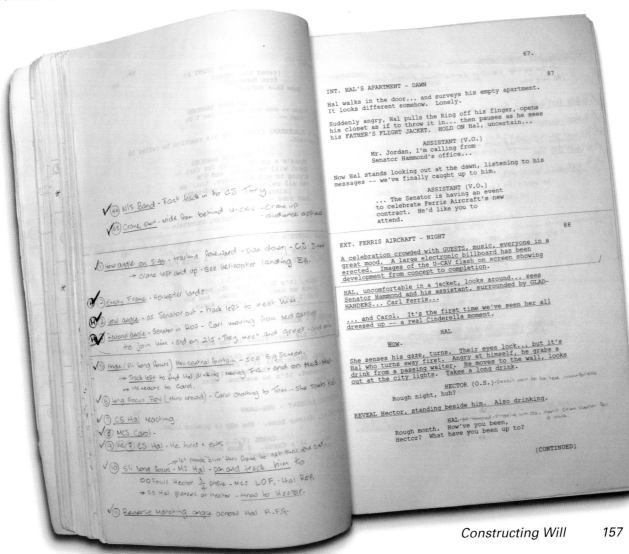

67.

87

INT. HAL'S APARTMENT - DAWN

Hal walks in the door... and surveys his empty apartment. It looks different somehow. Lonely.

Suddenly angry, Hal pulls the Ring off his finger, opens his closet as if to throw it in... then pauses as he sees his FATHER'S FLIGHT JACKET. HOLD ON Hal, uncertain...

                    ASSISTANT (V.O.)
          Mr. Jordan, I'm calling from
          Senator Hammond's office...

Now Hal stands looking out at the dawn, listening to his messages -- we've finally caught up to him.

                    ASSISTANT (V.O.)
          ... The Senator is having an event
          to celebrate Ferris Aircraft's new
          contract. He'd like you to
          attend.

                                              88

EXT. FERRIS AIRCRAFT - NIGHT

A celebration crowded with GUESTS, music, everyone in a great mood. A large electronic billboard has been erected. Images of the U-CAV flash on screen showing development from concept to completion.

HAL, uncomfortable in a jacket, looks around... sees Senator Hammond and his assistant, surrounded by GLAD-HANDERS... Carl Ferris...

... and Carol. It's the first time we've seen her all dressed up -- a real Cinderella moment.

                    HAL
          Wow.

She senses his gaze, turns. Their eyes lock... but it's Hal who turns away first. Angry at himself, he grabs a drink from a passing waiter. He moves to the wall, looks out at the city lights. Takes a long drink.

                    HECTOR (O.S.)
          Rough night, huh?

REVEAL Hector, standing beside him. Also drinking.

                    HAL
          Rough month. How've you been,
          Hector? What have you been up to?

                                        (CONTINUED)

PART III

SELECTING HECTOR

Left: Hector Hammond. Photo by François Duhamel.

Below: Coast City College graphic by Amanda Hunter with Zachary Zirlin.

Ever since writer John Broome introduced him to comic book readers in 1961, Hector Hammond has remained one of Green Lantern's most notorious foes, but the character has continually evolved throughout the years. He was originally portrayed as a petty criminal whose deliberate contact with an irradiated meteor caused his head to grow disproportionately, bestowing him with mental telepathy and telekinetic powers. When comic book writer Geoff Johns reintroduced Hal Jordan to readers in *Green Lantern: Secret Origin,* he also updated the Hammond character, connecting his origin to Jordan's by establishing him as Dr. Hammond, a slick science consultant at Ferris Aircraft who unsuccessfully pines for Carol Ferris's affection. By a strange twist of fate, Hammond's powers are also attributed to Abin Sur; he acquires them from an accidental exposure to the meteorite powering the fallen Lantern's crashed vessel.

Although influenced by the new take on the character, the screenwriters took it further, adapting Hammond's origin to the context of the film. Rather than presenting him as a criminal or villain, they gave him a more complex personal history. Portrayed in the film by Peter Sarsgaard, Hammond is a nebbish science professor and childhood friend to Hal Jordan and Carol Ferris who not only lacks Jordan's confidence and personality, but also his own father's, an ambitious politician played by Tim Robbins. Hammond's introverted persona is then given an outlet when he's unexpectedly empowered by a mysterious yellow substance that triggers his dark and tragic descent into madness.

The set for Hector Hammond's apartment gave production designer Grant Major and set decorator Anne Kuljian the opportunity to provide more insight into the character. "His environment is his life, and it needed to feel closed in. He still lives in the same place he moved into when he was an undergraduate," explains Major. Sarsgaard met with Kuljian to discuss the character before she began dressing the set. "Peter wanted to make sure I wasn't presenting Hammond as a mad scientist, he's more complex than that. He felt the character had a much closer relationship with his mother than he did with his father, who never really understood or accepted him, contributing to his introverted, loner personality." Kuljian

Left: *Geoff Johns reintroduced Hector Hammond's character in the comics, turning him into a slick science consultant at Ferris Aircraft who unsuccessfully pines for Carol's affection. Johns's update also attributed Hammond's powers to Abin Sur; but unlike the film, he acquires them from an accidental exposure to the meteorite powering the fallen Lantern's vessel. Green Lantern no. 32 (August 2008). Text by Geoff Johns and art by Ivan Reis and Oclair Albert.*

Right, top: *Professor Hammond in his science lab at Coast City College. Photo by François Duhamel.*

Right, bottom: *For Hammond's apartment, set decorator Anne Kuljian worked with actor Peter Sarsgaard to provide more insight into the character. "His company are his things, and we just layered and layered and layered on Hector's personality through the dressing." Photo by François Duhamel.*

recalls assembling presentation boards for Sarsgaard. "It was fantastic to hear his ideas. We would go through it and he'd add certain things that he wanted, like a picture of his mother holding him as a small child. We wanted to make his desk area feel like he's always there; his multiple computers, his phone, his food, and his pets are all close by. You really wanted to get the feeling that Hector was pretty much always in his apartment by himself and never had guests, whereas with Hal's apartment it was the opposite. Hector's has much more clutter, much more furniture, and much more ambiance of a past. His company are his things, and we just layered and layered and layered on Hector's personality through the dressing."

Hammond's vast scientific expertise in the field of xenobiology appears to be what finally gains him some attention when he's selected by the government to conduct their initial physiological assessment of an earth-shattering discovery: the body of Abin Sur. As Kuljian notes, "When he's pulled into the Department of Extranormal Operations, you get a sense that this is the type of high-tech environment more befitting his expertise, but something he never had the [strength of] personality to accomplish on his own."

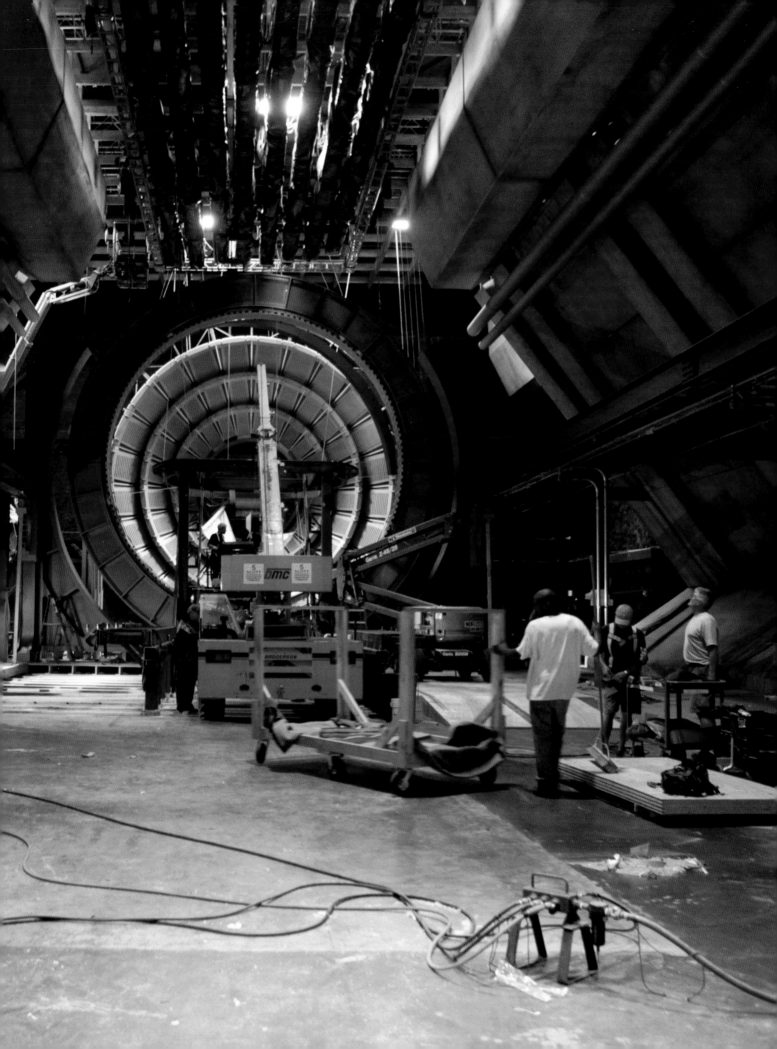

THE DEPARTMENT OF EXTRANORMAL OPERATIONS

Left: *The D.E.O. set under construction on stage one at Second Line Stages. Photo by Michele Moen.*

Below: *The D.E.O. logo was one of the hardest graphics to design says Amanda Hunter. "The all seeing eye was important to Grant [Major]. We went through many eyes before choosing the captivating engraving by Carl Joseph Meyer (1796-1856). It pulled you into the center graphic with a severity. The logo says government, while still maintaining its own unique language. However, we used it sparingly to keep it from going campy."*

It was originally scripted as an ambiguous secret government facility, presided over by a silver-haired scientist with the mysterious alias "Pipe," until co-producer Geoff Johns saw a golden opportunity to integrate the DC Universe and one of its more infamous characters into the film. Johns recommended turning the facility into the Department of Extranormal Operations (D.E.O.), a fictional government agency from the comics that monitors and protects the public from the unknown. To run the outfit, he suggested Dr. Amanda Waller, a character introduced by John Ostrander in the 1980s. Waller's tragic backstory was researched extensively for the film, and a sequence of comic book panels were meticulously reproduced as a series of flashbacks that pay full homage to the origins of the fiery character.

The D.E.O. underground installation where the government is holding Abin Sur's lifeless body was initially conceptualized as a freestanding, multilevel glass structure situated deep within a rocky cave, but as production designer Grant Major recalls, "it still wasn't quite as bold of a design." Director Martin Campbell wanted to emerge from a compressed underground tunnel and reveal a space that instantly impressed, evoking the scope and grandeur that made production designer Ken Adam's classic James Bond sets so memorable. The underground lab set needed to be an alluring contrast to Hector Hammond's own humble, cluttered environment, and provide a large-scale canvas for a major action sequence between Green Lantern and Hammond.

Major remembers scouting the New Orleans area in hopes of finding a dream location to build the set. Then they came across NASA's Michoud Assembly Facility. The 832-acre site is one of the largest manufacturing plants in the world, and where the space shuttle's familiar orange external fuel tanks were once manufactured. "They took us into this massive building where they pressure-tested the external tanks, and it had this great big 'O' shape at the end." Although the location wasn't used for filming, the ring motif left an indelible impression on Major. He integrated the bold graphic shape into the design of the set, and even gave it a purpose. A pivotal scene that called for Hammond to conduct an alien autopsy on Abin

Above and right: *Comic book panels from writer John Ostrander's 1987* Secret Origins *no. 14 (above), featured the Suicide Squad and told Amanda Waller's life-altering origin story. Art by Luke McDonnell and Dave Hunt. Actress Angela Bassett, who portrays Waller (right), recreates the scene on a bluescreen stage. Photo by Rosa Palomo.*

Above right: *Amanda Waller's high security D.E.O. badge. Graphics by Amanda Hunter with Zachary Zirlin.*

Top: *Summoned to an undisclosed underground facility (top left), Hammond's skills are about to be put to the test by Waller (top right).*

Above: *Digital rendering of the D.E.O. set by William Hunter and Rodolfo Damaggio.*

Sur was revised to depict a more probable noninvasive, high-tech, forensic procedure, making full use of the 'O' shaped ring as a massive MRI scan.

Lead set designer William Hunter, whose involvement on the set lasted for six straight months, is credited by Major as being one of the principal contributors to what became the film's largest fully contained built environment. The two-story 120 x 100-foot lab set filled the largest soundstage at Second Line Stages, and the D.E.O.'s covert entrance and tunnels took up half of another stage. Major wanted the massive lab space to lead the viewer's eye directly to the larger-than-life glowing ring with Abin Sur's body on the gurney suspended in the center.

"The lab needed to be designed in perspective, from a very specific walking approach, so it was important to design it with the camera lens in mind," says Hunter, who rendered the set using a computer even though his background is architecture and traditional hand drawing. "While this work can be done with hand drawings, modeling a set like this digitally in 3-D is incredibly efficient. It tells you how large in scale a space needs to be to have an impact, where the design emphasis should be, and where you can cut back," explains Hunter. He began by exploring the spatial conditions around the ring, which ultimately came in at 35 feet in diameter. "We looked at many options and actions that would allow a suspended and fully contained 'sterile' area for the autopsy to take place in. I ended up working out a machine, rigged by special effects, which allowed the floor to move up into a clear suspended bubble at the ring's center." To fabricate the clear dome, construction coordinator John Hoskins worked with one of the world's premiere manufacturers of room-sized aquariums. The clear acrylic half-sphere, which was 18 feet in diameter, was built with removable panels to allow for camera access. It arrived just in time —one week before shooting.

"Lighting was also a big driver in the underground lab," notes set decorator Anne Kuljian, who worked closely with Major and cinematographer Dion Beebe to integrate their lighting design into the set. She added a number of practical fixtures, such as the lighting cubes on the floor and the long tubular fixtures that hang on both sides of the corridors, which Major used as a path of light to help drive the viewers eye towards the LED illuminated ring.

When it came time for Campbell to plot out the complex action sequence, he and stunt coordinator Gary Powell made full use of the set, even incorporating the robotic arms on either side of the observation booth, which Major had placed merely to imply functionality. Suddenly, they too had become a major part of the action in what would become one of the film's more memorable sets.

Above: *Early studies of the underground facility by Grant Major.*

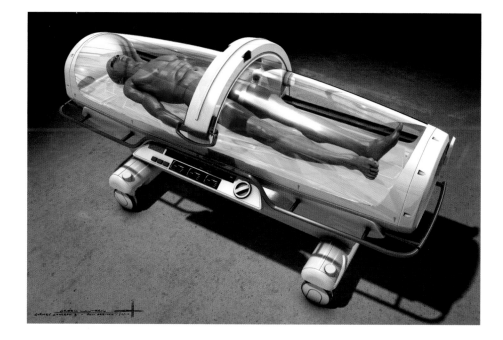

Above left: *An intricate retinal scanner for the high security installation. Concept illustration by Paul Ozzimo.*

Above right: *Study model of the D.E.O. lab by Brett Phillips. Photo by Brett Phillips.*

Left: *Concept of the gurney that preserves the remains of Abin Sur. Illustration by Paul Ozzimo.*

Below: *An earlier version of the script had Hammond conducting a full alien autopsy on the body. Concept illustration by Paul Ozzimo.*

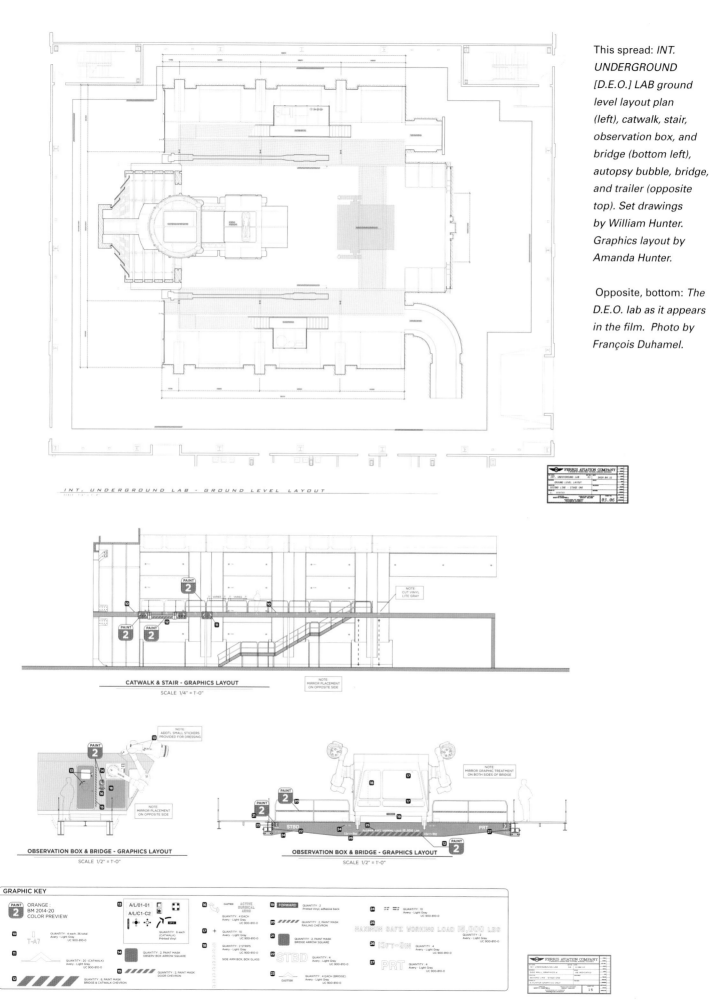

This spread: *INT. UNDERGROUND [D.E.O.] LAB ground level layout plan (left), catwalk, stair, observation box, and bridge (bottom left), autopsy bubble, bridge, and trailer (opposite top). Set drawings by William Hunter. Graphics layout by Amanda Hunter.*

Opposite, bottom: The D.E.O. lab as it appears in the film. Photo by François Duhamel.

INT. UNDERGROUND LAB - GROUND LEVEL LAYOUT

CATWALK & STAIR - GRAPHICS LAYOUT
SCALE 1/4" = 1'-0"

OBSERVATION BOX & BRIDGE - GRAPHICS LAYOUT
SCALE 1/2" = 1'-0"

OBSERVATION BOX & BRIDGE - GRAPHICS LAYOUT
SCALE 1/2" = 1'-0"

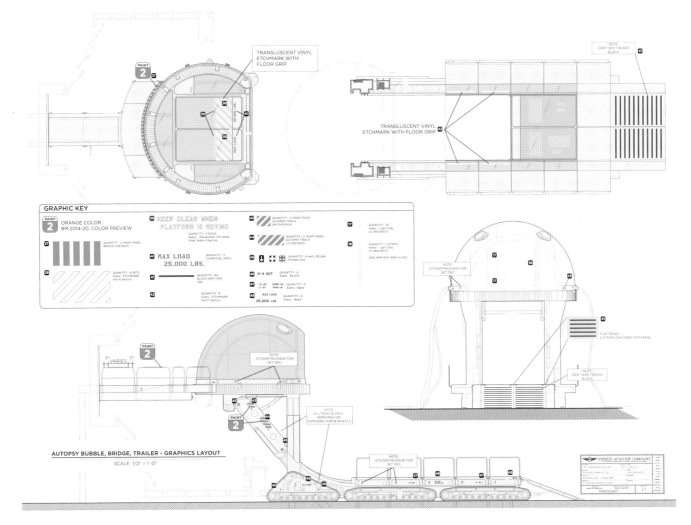

He levitates up to stand on the gurney.

The Senator and Waller back away.

Hector stares at them in fury.

They turn and make a run for it.

Hector's eyes flash yellow.

A cabinet (or whatever) skates across the floor --

-- tripping them both.

The guards raise their taser guns and fire at Hector --

-- who deflects the electrical blasts straight back at them --

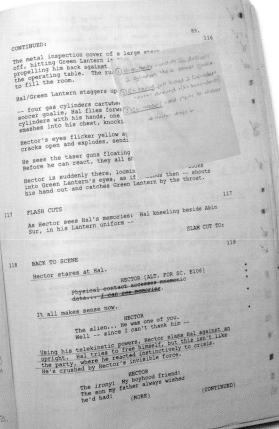

-- dropping them to the floor, poleaxed.

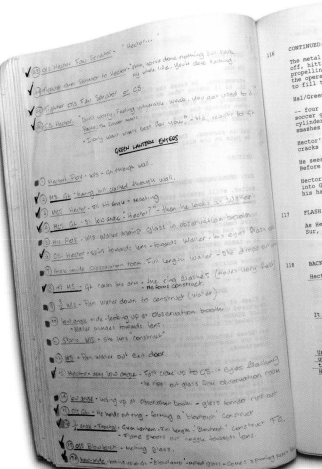

This spread: *Storyboard excerpts, BUNKER FIGHT sequence (Scene 114 / Shots 210-290 / March 23, 2010) Storyboard artist: Collin Grant.*

Left: *Director Martin Campbell's film script with his handwritten notes breaking down the shots for the BUNKER FIGHT sequence. Photo by Ozzy Inguanzo.*

HARNESSING FEAR

Left: *Hector channels his fear.*

Below: *Hammond's massive comic book likeness, from* Green Lantern: Secret Origin. *Art by Ivan Reis.*

The process of realizing Hector Hammond's large-headed comic book likeness for the live-action film began half a year prior to casting the role. The script required the character to undergo an emotional and physical transformation throughout the course of the film. The emotional transformation would eventually be entrusted to actor Peter Sarsgaard, who would play it to eerie perfection. For the physical transformation, director Martin Campbell wanted a gradual, yet visceral metamorphosis that looked absolutely credible.

Creature designer Aaron Sims and his team studied various head sizes. "It ultimately came down to face proportion versus head proportion, basically a small face inside of a gigantic head. At first we stayed as true as possible to the comics, but a head that gigantic and functional is just hard to take seriously, so we steered toward what worked best for the film," he says. They produced over thirty illustrations, each representing a different stage of growth and deterioration. Four were chosen. "I think moving toward a more mutated feel, where the head is asymmetrical and diseased, was the most effective way to go. It detracts from the comedic aspect associated with such a huge head," explains Sims, who then handed them over to prosthetic makeup effects department head Joel Harlow.

Harlow initially sculpted four clay maquettes representing each of Sims's head growth stages. Campbell then requested a fifth, massive stage, recalls Harlow. "He wanted to push the envelope and make one as big as possible, then scale back from that. Once we decided how big we were going to go, I took a photo of Peter [Sarsgaard] and superimposed the maquette sculptures over the top of his head." The multiple images of the actor were then printed out full scale and posted along the corridor in the makeup lab. "We could now see what they would look like with his body proportions, and how far we'd have to build the neck out. The biggest concern when dealing with a character like Hector is that it can easily look like a giant light bulb or a Q-tip, so we balanced that out with the neck and all those facial imperfections," explains Harlow. In addition to Hector's trademark mustache, Harlow's team added beard stubble and gave him long greasy hair. "There's so much skin when you get that large, you need

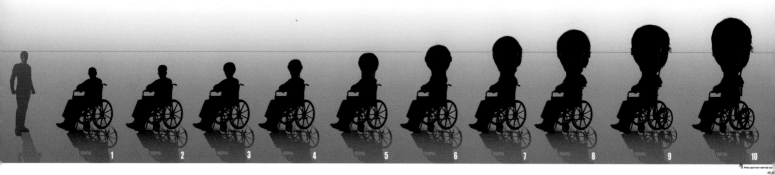

something to break it up and help sell the fact that it's not just a guy buried under a giant rubber head," he says.

In designing the makeup, Harlow and his team also made sure Sarsgaard's performance wasn't buried either. "We tried to keep the pieces as thin as possible around his face so he could still emote through them. Some sculptural elements needed to be there to sell the character, but the silicon we used was very soft, so even if there were thick areas it would still translate. Then it's a matter of Peter wearing the pieces and looking at the mirror to see what sort of expressions he could make with them and determining how far he had to go to sell what he wanted to sell," explains Harlow.

The final stage makeup was made up of nine silicon pieces, each prepainted and applied in layers onto Sarsgaard's skin. The artists blended the pieces together with paint and then added the hairpieces, mustache, and individual beard stubbles. The meticulous three-hour process began around 3:00 a.m. every morning. "Even though we tried to make these pieces as light as possible, it's still an uncomfortable process, especially having to hold your head up under something that big. I've been told by many actors that this process of transforming into a character helps get them into the role. Hector's transformation in the film is painful and uncomfortable, so hopefully you get somebody like Peter who can use that," says Harlow.

For the fear-based Yellow Energy that radiates out from Hector, production designer Grant Major turned to energy guru Seth Engstrom. "When we were creating the look of Green Energy, we got many distinct patterns by shining a laser through different objects. In doing that, we noticed that certain rocks gave us jagged, cross-section patterns that were sharper and more vicious than others. The laser light was picking up all the cracks and fissures within the rocks and projecting them outward," recalls Engstrom. Those harsh patterns ultimately informed his overall design approach and became the basis for the yellow energy signature. "Both the green and yellow energy were born out of the same process, yet reflect different characteristics. Like our physical experiments with the rocks, the quality of the light is reflective of the character they shine through."

"Grant and I also spoke about the idea of the 'energy from within,'" he continues. "If this yellow energy were inside Hector, what would it look like emanating from his head? I always thought of Green Energy inhabiting your heart and Yellow Energy infecting your mind, like a bad case of brain freeze." To sell the concept, Engstrom produced a series of renderings that showed a range of energy intensities emanating from within Hector's visage. "At first you see just a bit coming through the eyes, but as he gets angrier, the light gets brighter. I thought it'd be cool to illuminate his skull from within and help show he's being consumed by something evil."

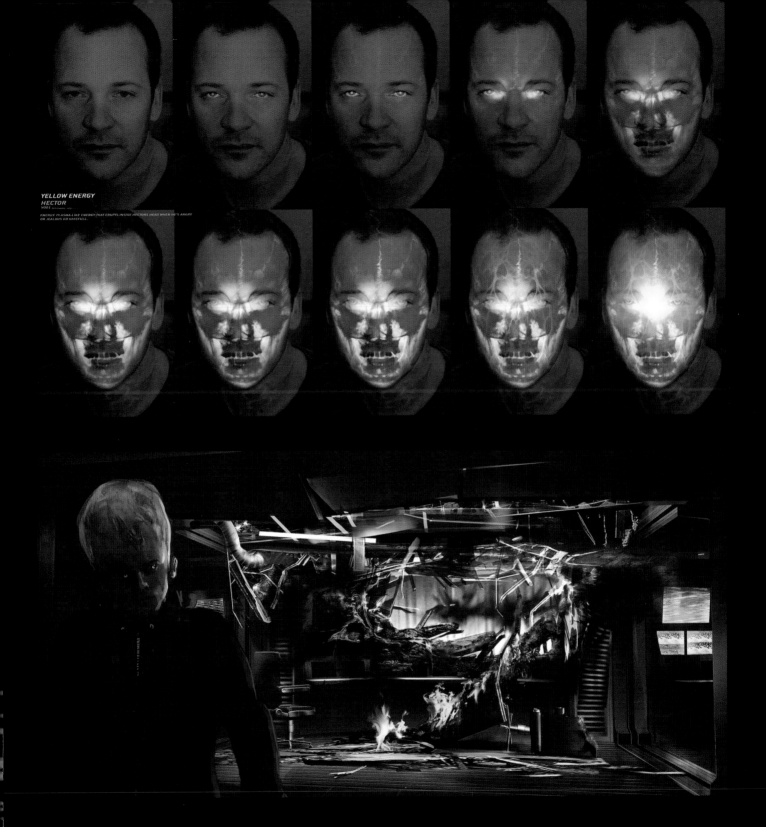

YELLOW ENERGY
HECTOR
V001
ENERGY-PLASMA-LIKE ENERGY THAT ERUPTS INSIDE HECTOR'S HEAD WHEN HE'S ANGRY
OR JEALOUS OR HATEFULL.

Top: *Using a photo of actor Peter Sarsgaard, concept illustrator Seth Engstrom conceptualized the progressive stages of Yellow Energy percolating within Hector's head.*

Above: *Hector's aftermath. Concept illustration by Paul Christopher.*

Above: *Early character concepts by The Aaron Sims Company.*

Right: *Through the use of stunt wires, Hector finally stands up to his father, an influential politician played by Tim Robbins. Photo by François Duhamel.*

HECTOR-13

Above left: *This illustration by The Aaron Sims Company became the foundation on which prosthetics makeup effects department head Joel Harlow based Hector's transformation. "I think moving toward a more mutated feel, where the head is more asymmetrical and diseased, was the most effective way to go. It detracted from the comedic aspect associated with such a huge head," explains Sims.*

Above and left: *After a three-hour process, actor Peter Sarsgaard is fully transformed by the prosthetics makeup effects team. Top photo courtesy Joel Harlow. Bottom photo by François Duhamel.*

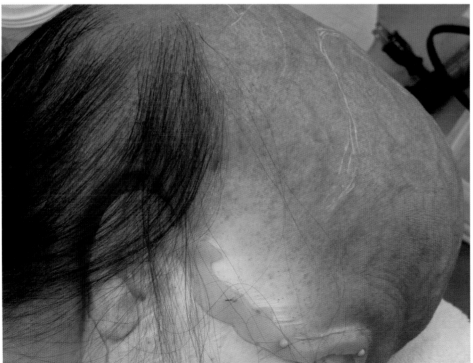

Above: *Joel Harlow sculpts Hector Hammond's enlarged head in clay. Photo courtesy Joel Harlow.*

Left: *Hector Hammond's silicon head appliance. Photo courtesy Joel Harlow.*

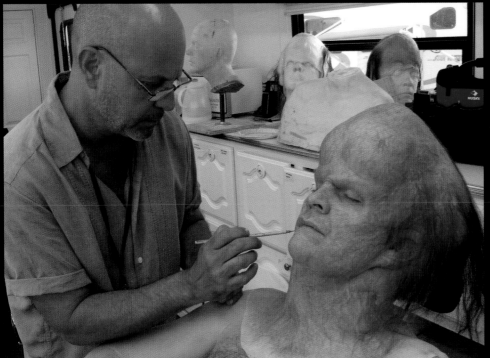

Above: *Harlow's series of maquettes showing Hector's stages of growth. A fifth, massive stage on the far right, was entertained by director Martin Campbell, but ultimately discarded. Photo courtesy Joel Harlow.*

Left: *David Dupuis applies the finishing touches onto Sarsgaard's face in the make-up trailer. Photo courtesy Joel Harlow.*

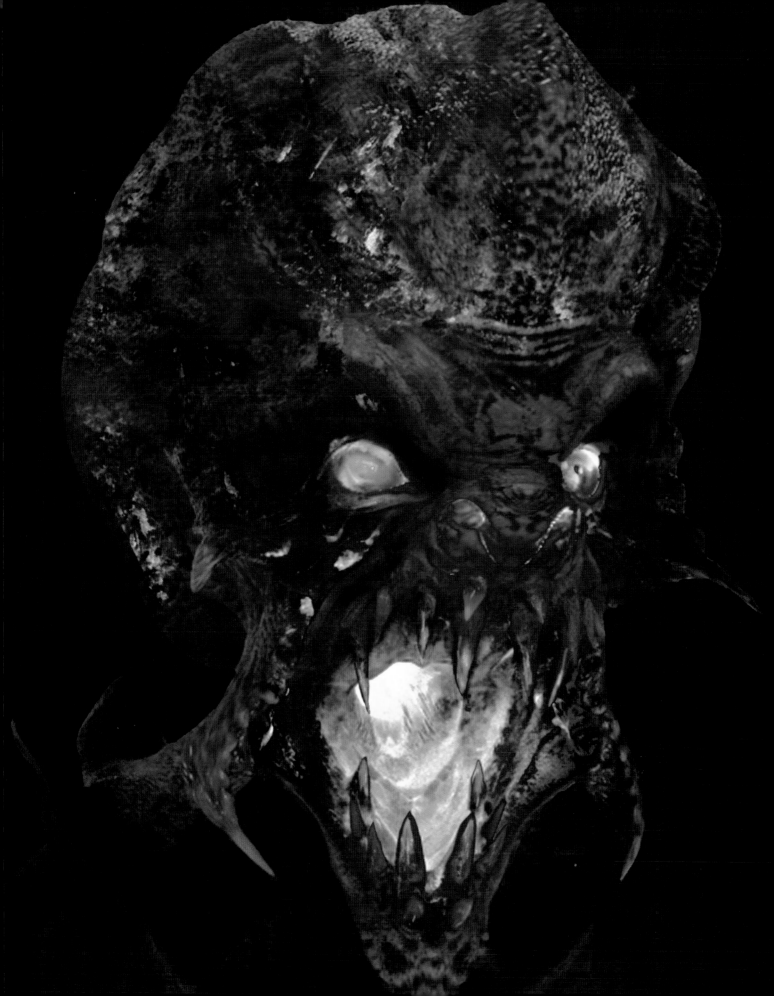

PARALLAX ATTACKS

The evil driving force behind the mysterious yellow energy is a vicious parasitic entity developed by comic book writer Geoff Johns in the 2004 miniseries *Green Lantern: Rebirth*. In it, Parallax is the physical embodiment of fear; a creature that dates back to the dawn of existence, and which has played a significant role in the mythology of the Green Lantern story throughout the years, infecting Hal Jordan and the guardian Ganthet in two popular story arcs.

In the film, the Guardians of the Universe are silent about Parallax's origin and true destructive nature. It's a secret so dangerous that it's never been disclosed outside their council, even kept from the Green Lantern Corps. The movie reveals in flashback that countless millennia ago, a roiling, fear-based Yellow Energy had been locked away within the cavernous walls of a forbidden vault. Also contained inside the rocky tomb was a massive glyph in the shape of a nefarious symbol, one that comic book readers will instantly recognize. "A symbol that movie audiences will now get to know," says production designer Grant Major, referring to the fear symbol associated in the comics with the Sinestro Corps. A forthcoming villainous analogue to the Green Lantern Corps, led by the Hal Jordan's former mentor.

Excited by a multitude of comic book images, Major and concept artist Justin Sweet decided to model the vault's central glyph around the infamous graphic shape to give it more history. "I thought of the symbol as a device that the Guardians had invented to contain the yellow fear energy, in a somewhat similar fashion to how the Green Lantern symbol is associated with the green energy. It's as if the shapes of these symbols have some sort of physical properties and are able to contain these forces. I also quite liked the graphic nature of the symbol itself, and because of the prominent role it plays in the mythology, it's important for audiences to become familiar with it here," explains Major.

Sealed in the vault and entangled around the massive glyph, the Yellow Energy appeared to have been forever entombed by the Guardians of the Universe. "Without anyone around to feel fear or a host body to infect, the nebulous Yellow Energy was in its most weakened, dormant stage, and completely trapped," but as concept artist Seth Engstrom elaborates, "a presence nearby provided a chance for it to escape. Suddenly, the sinewy yellow energy's initial properties began to take on more jagged patterns, and as it consumed enough fear to finally break free from its confines, its true vicious characteristic is revealed, which is why we needed to design the energy to look like fear, to feel like fear." Now, traveling the cosmos unrestrained, Parallax has grown into a powerful and unstoppable threat to the Guardians and the Green Lantern Corps, as it consumes entire civilizations through terror and paranoia.

A massive artistic effort was undertaken to conceptualize, develop, and design the Parallax creature. Headed by Major and artists Sweet, Engstrom, and creature designer Neville Page, the ongoing design process continued into post-production. Major recalls early discussions in Los Angeles when director Martin Campbell referenced footage from the 9/11 terrorist attacks on New York City. "The images of those massive dust clouds coming down the streets from the collapsing World Trade Center towers are ingrained into the psyche of not only America, but the rest of the world, and they are directly associated with terror." The footage served as general direction for the feeling Campbell wanted to capture, but never meant to be taken literally, says the director. "The danger with Parallax is that it can easily become a great big yellow cloud, floating about the universe, gobbling up people on planets." Major adds, "No one wanted to do a cloud or dust creature. Not only have they been done in previous films, they typically come off as non-tangible and unthreatening. Out of our library of research books, I had seen some fantastic images of India, from a festival where people are covered in paint, just fantastic pictures of this writhing mass of people. Putting those two references together is where the concept design for Parallax was born. These massive cloud-like tentacles, not of dust, but of tangible, writhing alien beings."

According to Major, the concept solidified when concept artist Justin Sweet began to channel renowned fantasy painter Zdzislaw Beksinski in his illustrations. "The creature's tentacles became a dried-up textural mash-up of these consumed alien beings, their life sucked out of them through fear, leaving their empty husks shrouding Parallax, like Dracula behind his cloak," he says. At an early Parallax concept meeting, Campbell was also struck by Sweet's ideas and his haunting imagery, "Really, Parallax is Justin's concept. He developed it and provided the images which gave us all a clue to the monster." Sweet recalls, "I did a forward shot looking right into this wave of lost souls and alien heads. That was the first one I did that Martin looked at and said, 'That's it!' From then on I kind of became the go-to guy for Parallax." But after months of designing fear incarnate, the work began to take a toll on the artist. "I'd spend all day playing really intense music while I worked, and I'd be immersed in these gloomy and horrible images of mummies and victims. Day in and day out of that stuff and you really start to feel lost and soulless, and my wife was starting to get concerned. So I was relieved when the time came to pass the baton over to the next guy," he says.

The next guy was Engstrom, who began the process of integrating his yellow energy concepts into Sweet's overall design of the creature, just as he had done previously with Hector Hammond. But there was one crucial piece that still needed work: the head of the monster. For that, Major called back creature designer Neville Page. "Initially I was very inspired by some of the images of Parallax from the Green Lantern comics. Although this incarnation of the character is not something you can point to directly in the comics, we did many variations on a theme. The starting point was

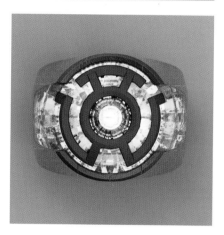

Above: *Concept design for the Yellow Power Ring by Joe Hiura. It retains the same design language as the Green Lantern Power Ring, while incorporating the iconic fear symbol.*

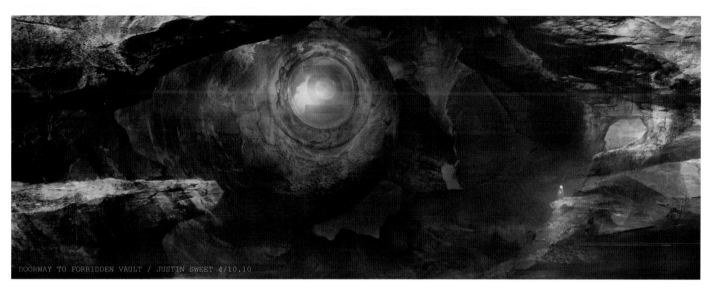

DOORWAY TO FORBIDDEN VAULT / JUSTIN SWEET 4/10.10

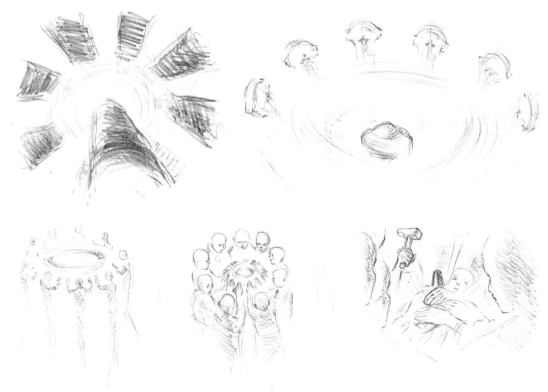

Top: *Locked away within the cavernous walls of the forbidden vault, the Yellow "fear-based" Energy swirls around a massive glyph in the shape of the infamous fear symbol. Concept art by Justin Sweet.*

Above: *The hidden, sealed entrance to the forbidden vault by Justin Sweet.*

Left: *Early concept sketches by Grant Major of the Guardians forging the Yellow Ring.*

Above: *A lone Guardian stares blindly into the brilliant yellow energy. Concept illustration by Justin Sweet.*

Right: *The attack. Concept illustration by Seth Engstrom.*

Left: *Various concept studies of Parallax in space by Justin Sweet.*

Above: *This painting of Parallax by Justin Sweet, sold Martin Campbell on the concept. "That was the first one I did that Martin looked at and said, 'That's it!' From then on I kind of became the go-to guy for Parallax," recalls Sweet.*

always the inside of the mouth, which is unique and emblematic of Parallax in the comics. So you could say that I designed the creature from the uvula out," he quips.

With concept designs in hand, it was up to visual effects supervisor Jim Berney and his team at Sony Pictures Imageworks to ultimately realize the monstrous creature through the use of digital effects. Over the course of several months, they began the process of building, texturing, and rigging a 3-D model of the beast, which would be animated, lit, and composited into the filmed footage of downtown Coast City for the climactic showdown between Fear and Willpower.

The downtown battle sequence, known by the visual effects sequence code: LP (Lantern fights Parallax), kept director Martin Campbell and veteran storyboard artists Collin Grant and Eric Ramsey actively storyboarding into the last days of shooting. Pixel Liberation Front's pre-visualization team, led by Kyle Robinson, would then work with the director to bring the LP storyboards (among other sequences) to life by animating their in-house digital models and incorporating them into the filmed footage. By the time principal photography on *Green Lantern* wrapped in New Orleans on August 6, 2010, Campbell had storyboarded more than twenty-one sequences, and most of them were "pre-vised." Ramsey recalls a conversation he had with Campbell about his previous film, *Edge of Darkness*. "I remember telling him how tight I thought the action was, how well it all just seemed to flow, and that it must have been very carefully planned out, and he said to me, 'Oh, darling, I leave nothing to chance.'"

Back in New Orleans, the veteran director would arrive at work early every morning, hours before anyone else. All alone in his office, he'd design each sequence, plan out each shot. Ramsey elaborates, "A lot of times on movies these days, you'll get a sheet of paper with a fragment of a scene or a paragraph and they'll ask you to just make up the storyboards. Then they'll discuss it and refine it, but it's different working for Martin. He's more involved with the storyboards than any director I've worked for in years. He knows what he wants and is really directing the movie, basically."

A huge admirer of director David Lean, known for classic epics such as *Lawrence of Arabia* and *The Bridge on the River Kwai*, Campbell sites the filmmaker's influence on his work, "Getting scope into a movie was something Lean was wonderful at doing. The amount of detail he puts into his work, the way he constructs it, the way shoots it. When there's somebody you admire, and you admire his work and know his movies, somehow it rubs off into you. I'll often do wide shots and I'll often pull the camera back. I like to see action wide; I like to know what is happening in the action. I don't like the idea of shooting everything close with a lot of offscreen bangs, you know? I like to see the choreography and get back with the camera."

Collin Grant, who has storyboarded for Campbell on several films, says he's one of the most disciplined directors he's ever worked with. "Once Martin figures out the sequence, he writes up his shot list and calls us into his office to go through it shot by shot." The director would sometimes block the action using an assortment of Green Lantern action figures, other times he'd line up the storyboard artists themselves and position himself where the camera would be. "We'd do a thumbnail sketch of the shot and show it to him, then he'd say, 'Oh no, darling, just a little bit tighter.' Once he'd approve it then we'd go back and draw it out fully,'" explains Ramsey. "He's very particular about what he wants," adds Grant. "He doesn't want to waste any time overshooting, and the storyboards illustrate exactly where the camera is going to be and what he needs to get on the day."

Campbell explains his process, "Storyboarding very simply is like writing the script. I always think of it in terms of cuts. I edit with the

Above: *This concept illustration of Parallax by Justin Sweet conveys a sense of scale and shows Green Lantern undeterred by the massive creature.*

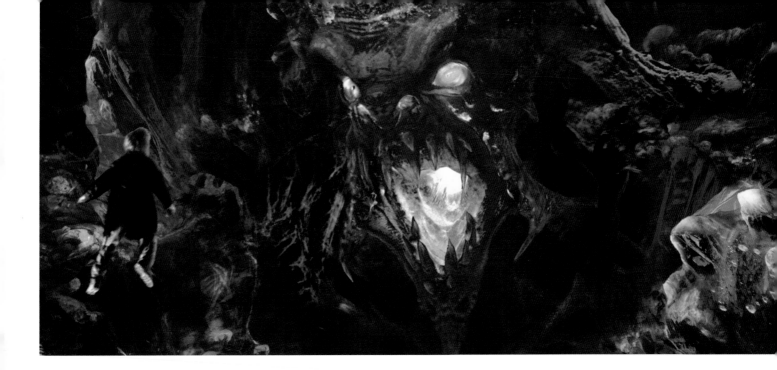

Top: *Hector communes with Parallax. Concept illustration by Seth Engstrom. Parallax head designed by Neville Page.*

Above: *Parallax approaching. Concept illustration by Paul Christopher.*

storyboards, I sort of cut the film together with them. And you'll probably find that if you look at the storyboards and look at the film, an awful lot is literally as per the storyboards. I may change the shot slightly, but I pretty much stick to them."

During a visit to the Ferris Aircraft set, Ramsey recalls an idyllic moment that sums up the experience for many who worked on the film. "I remember looking into the video assist monitor at the framing. The set looked beautiful, the composition of the shot was exactly what we had drawn in the storyboards, and Martin was on set and in command, very charming, yet very direct—it was fantastic! His work ethic was just phenomenal, and it inspired all of us to meet the challenge and to put out our best work."

Above: *This terrifying illustration of the beast by Justin Sweet captured the feeling of sheer terror that director Martin Campbell wanted to reproduce on film.*

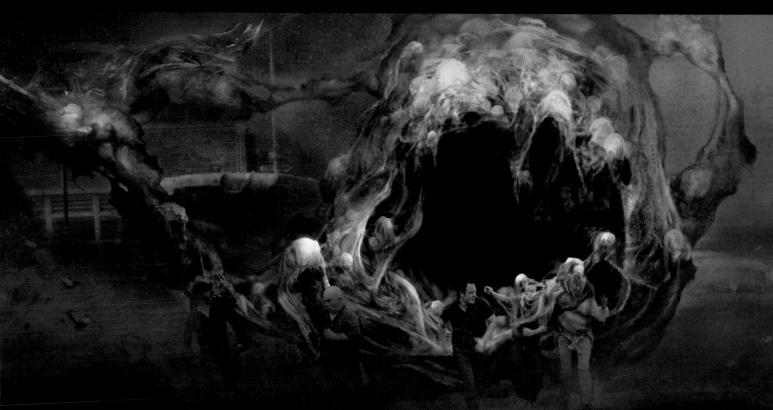

Top: *Early concept of Parallax's tentacles swooping down a street, consuming frightened residents of Coast City. Art by Justin Sweet.*

Above: *Justin Sweet illustrated Parallax's tentacles devouring a small herd of Green Lantern art department staff. (Left to Right) William Hunter, Wright McFarland, Robert Johnson, Joe Hiura, and*

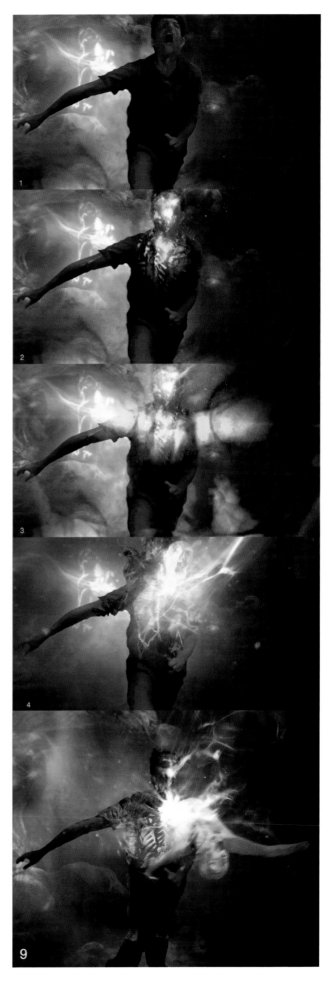

Above: *A side view of the tentacle attacking concept designer Fabian Lacey. Frightened in the background (right to left), William Hunter, Wright McFarland, and Robert Johnson. Concept illustration by Justin Sweet. Photo by Ozzy Inguanzo.*

Right: *This series of illustrations depicting a victim's soul being sucked out (far right) was "pre-vised" (near right) by the team from Pixel Liberation Front. Concept art by Seth Engstrom. Pre-vis courtesy Kyle Robinson.*

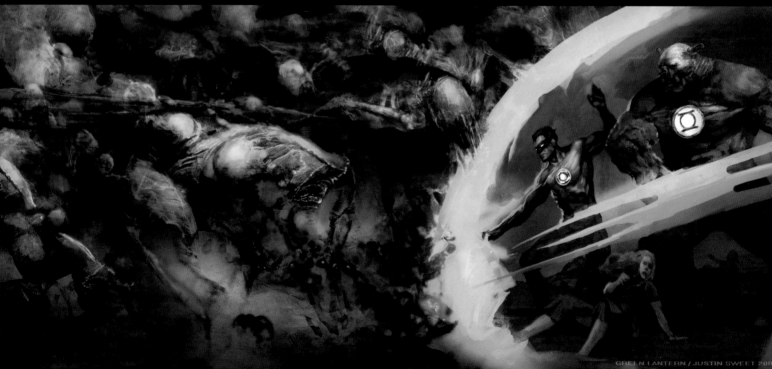

Above: *Early concept illustrations of the downtown battle by Justin Sweet.*

Opposite: *Hal Jordan's willpower is put to the test as he holds back Parallax with a shield construct. Concept illustrations by Seth Engstrom with Justin Sweet. Shield construct by James Clyne.*

SPACE FIELD - FROM THE INSIDE - v006

The school kids pour out of the bus, followed by the driver. We reveal that the bus has been in an accident. The CAMERA CRANES DOWN.

-- at the approaching tentacle.

The driver trips --

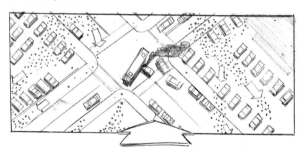

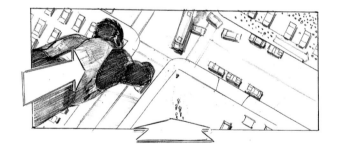

-- and falls.

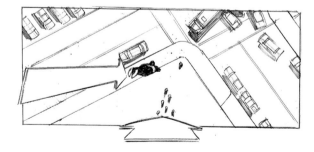

She turns and looks back in horror --

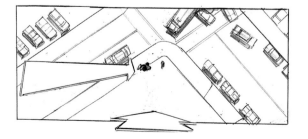

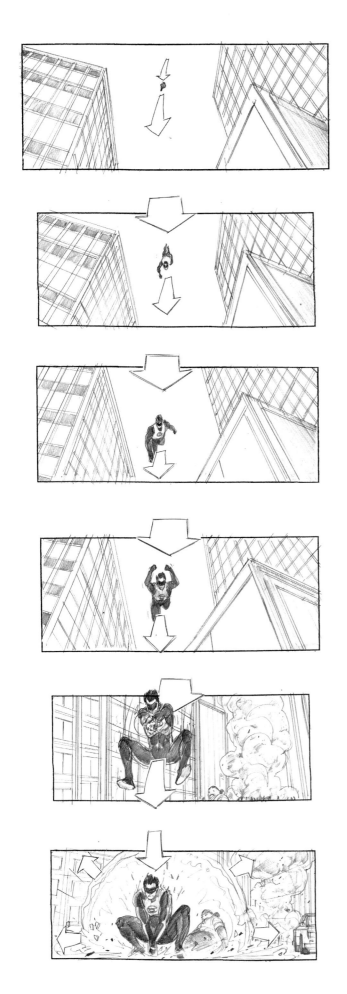

BOOOOMM!

BOOOOMM!

Green Lantern has arrived!

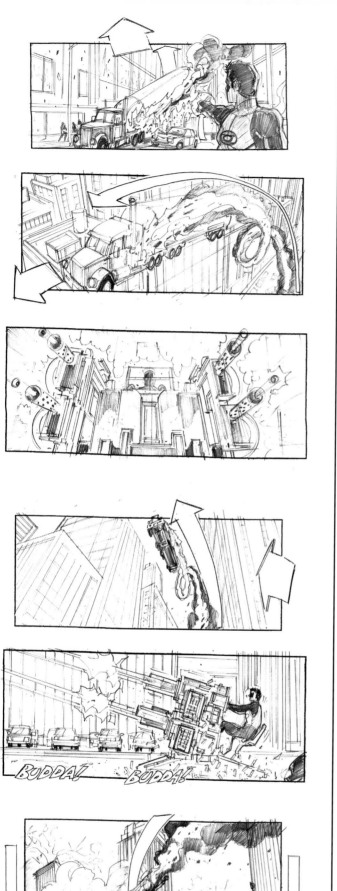

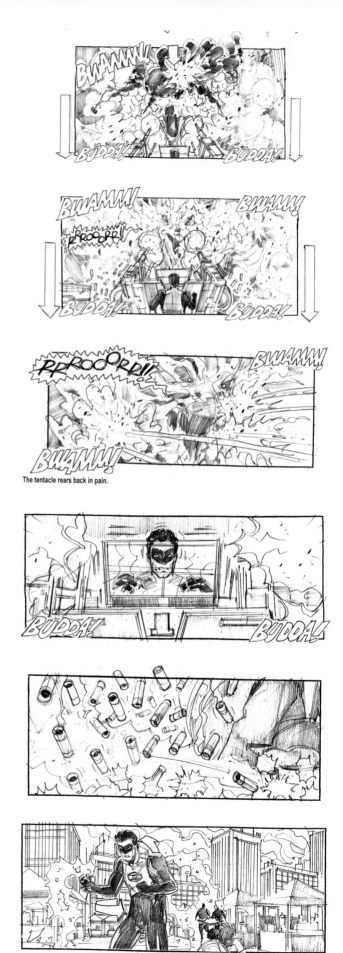

The tentacle rears back in pain.

Green Lantern helps the driver up and passes her to two other people.

Pages 198–200: *Storyboard excerpts, LANTERN FIGHTS PARALLAX sequence (Scenes A131-B136 / Shots 270-340 / July 28, 2010). Storyboard artist: Collin Grant.*

Left: *Jeff Julian initially proposed hurling a flaming fuel truck into Parallax in this concept illustration.*

Below: *Martin Campbell (left) describes a shot to storyboard artist Collin Grant.*

Bottom: *Green Lantern's massive automatic cannon construct by Jeff Julian.*

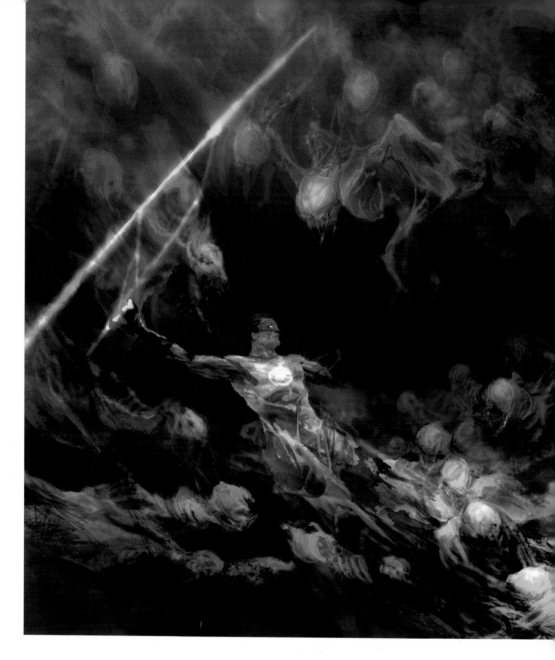

Right: *Prior to incorporating Neville Page's head design, Justin Sweet produced this powerful concept illustration of Hal Jordan facing-off against Parallax.*

Below: *Green Lantern faces his fears. Concept art by Justin Sweet.*

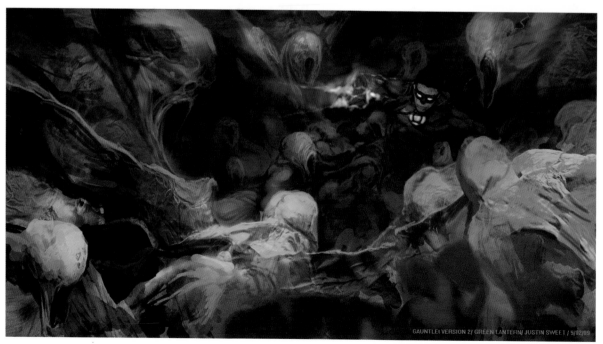

Right: *Director Martin Campbell composes a shot, surrounded by crew (left to right) Rick Chavez, Julian Wall, John Buckley, Jim Berney, Campbell, Bruce Moriarty, Dion Beebe, Sion Michel, Kent Houston, and Alex Bicknell.*

This spread: *Green Lantern bursts up through the stratosphere. Concept illustration by Michele Moen. Storyboard panel by Eric Ramsey.*

Big Moose, LLC.
Production Office
1231 Prytania St. 4th floor
New Orleans, LA 70130
Office: 504-523-2200 Fax: 504-523-9883

Director: Martin Campbell
Producer: Donald De Line, Greg Berlanti
Exec. Producer: Herb Gains
Co-Producer: Lucienne Papon
Writers: Greg Berlanti, Michael Green, Marc Guggenheim
Bill Broyles, Michael Goldenberg

Courtesy Breakfast Van Leaves Embassy Suites @ 6:48AM

CREW CALL

7:18am Lv
7:30am rpt

DATE: Friday, August 6, 2010
DAY: Day 102 of 100

SHOOTING CALL: 8am

WEATHER: Clouds at times, 50% Chance of rain
HI- 91   Lo- 79

SUNRISE: 6:20am   SUNSET: 7:52pm
DAWN: 5:55am   DUSK: 8:17pm

SAFETY FIRST
A full copy of the safety program will be on file with the A.D.s at all times.

*** No forced calls without prior approval from the UPM, all crew must NDB- No Exceptions!!! ***

SET / DESCRIPTION	SCENE	D/N	CAST #	PGS.	SET
LAST DAY TO MAKE DONATIONS FOR NEW ORLEANS MISSION FOR THE HOMELESS					
INT GREEN SPHERE-HAL'S RIDE-BLUESCREEN					STAGE 1
Hal's Wild ride in Green Sphere....	31-1	Eve 3	1, 1x	3/8	80-1, 2, 3, 90-1, 110-1, 2
Green Sphere comes to a dead stop...Hal thrown on his back...Sphere vanishes..He drops	31-5	N3	1, 1x	1/8	140-1 thru 6
EXT MILITARY CEMETERY-OA-BLUESCREEN					
GL joins Sinestro....Graves of Lanterns killed by Parallax...GL realizes Parallax has infected the Earth	124-1	space 8	1, 4	7/8	
Tomar-Re joins them.....Your world is finished.....Guardians are forging a new weapon	124-2	space 8	1, 4	4/8	
Sinestro & Tomar-Re remind GL he is a Green Lantern & Must adhere to the orders...GL going to see Guardians	B125-1	space 8	1, 4	1 3/8	
				TOTAL PGS: 3 2/8	

YOU ARE ALL AWESOME WOULD GO TO WAR WITH ANY ONE OF YOU ANYTIME— THANK YOU THANK YOU THANK YOU Herb GG

CAST	ST	CHARACTER	MAKE UP	COSTUME	SET CALL	PICK-UP	TRANSPORTATION
1. Harold Jordan	WF	Hal Jordan	7:15am	-	8am	7am pick up	P/U @ Residence to Base at Stage
4. Mark Strong	WF	Sinestro	5am	-	9:30am	4:45am pick up	P/U @ Loews to Base at Stage
Gary Powell	WF	Stunt Coordinator	-	-	per GP	-	Self Drive
Lee Morrison	WF	Stunt	-	-	per GP	-	Self Drive
1x. Daniel Stevens	WF	Hal Stunt Double	-	-	per GP	-	Self Drive
Nikki Berwick	WF	Stunt	-	-	per GP	-	Self Drive
4x. Sam Hargrave	WF	Sinestro Stunt Double	-	-	per GP	-	Self Drive
45x. Dorian Kingi	WF	Stunt	-	-	per GP	8:30am pick up	P/U @ Residence Inn to Base at Stage

STAND-INS	REPORT	SET
1 Hal	6:45am	7am
1 Sinestro	8:15am	8:30am

Thank you! Bunch's Bruce

TOTAL BG: 0   TOTAL S.I.: 2

ART DEPT/SET DEC: Artwork for Sequence on hand, Bluescreen *platforms*
PROPS: GL ring
V F/X: Witness Cams, Bluescreen, GL, Sinestro, Tomar-Re suits, Green Energy Sphere
S F/X: Compressed Air movers, e-fans, green energy wind on Hal's hair
STUNT COORDINATOR: Hal Harness, Sinestro Harness, Tomar-Re Harness, Hal's Wild Ride, Rubber Zorb, Hal Stunt double
HEALTH/SAFETY: Ambulance at 7am
LOCATIONS: A/C as required, Stage Manager
GRIP/ELECTRIC: Technocranes, Bluescreen
MAKE UP/HAIR: Tracking Markers
PROSTHETICS: Tracking Markers, Sinestro lenses
COSTUMES: GL, Tomar-Re, GL stunt Dbl
ADDL CREW: Stage Manager, lens tech

Thank you so much for such a wonderful shoot. You are an utterly fantastic crew! Martin Campbell

IN BRIGHTEST DAY IN BLACKEST NIGHT GREEN LANTERNS CAST & CREW ROCKS IT RIGHT!!!!

I was 12 when I started this film. Thank you, one and all— for an incredible effort! What a crew... what a film. Love, Ryan Reynolds

THANK YOU CAST & CREW FOR ALL YOUR HARD WORK...CONGRATULATIONS!

Thanks to the most excellent dedicated, hardworking and talented crew. You are all worthy of the ring. See ya on OA, love, Donald

UNIT PRODUCTION MANAGER: Neri Kyle Tannenbaum	1ST ASSISTANT DIRECTOR: Bruce Moriarty
PRODUCTION SUPERVISOR: Sara Flamm	2ND ASSISTANT DIRECTOR: Trish Stanard
	2ND 2ND ASSISTANT DIRECTOR: Mikey Eberle

IN BRIGHTEST DAY . . .

IN BLACKEST NIGHT . . .

NO EVIL SHALL ESCAPE MY SIGHT

LET THOSE WHO WORSHIP EVIL'S MIGHT

BEWARE MY POWER—

GREEN LANTERN'S LIGHT!